UNDERSTANDING WRITING TRANSFER

UNDERSTANDING WRITING TRANSFER

Implications for Transformative Student Learning in Higher Education

EDITED BY

Jessie L. Moore and Randall Bass

FOREWORD BY

Betsy O. Barefoot and John N. Gardner

Sty/us

STERLING, VIRGINIA

Sty/us

Published by Stylus Publishing, LLC.
22883 Quicksilver Drive
Sterling, Virginia 20166-2102

Library of Congress Cataloging-in-Publication Data
Names: Bass, Randall, editor. | Moore, Jessie L., editor.
Title: Understanding writing transfer: implications for
transformative student learning in higher education/
edited Randall Bass and Jessie L. Moore.
Description: Sterling, Virginia : Stylus Publishing, LLC, [2017] |
Includes bibliographical references and index.
Identifiers: LCCN 2016022685 (print) |
LCCN 2016041186 (ebook) |
ISBN 9781620365847 (cloth : alk. paper) |
ISBN 9781620365854 (pbk. : alk. paper) |
ISBN 9781620365861 (library networkable e-edition) |
ISBN 9781620365878 (consumer e-edition)
Subjects: LCSH: English language--
Rhetoric--Study and teaching (Higher) |
Academic writing--Study and teaching (Higher) |
Language arts--Correlation with content subjects. |
Interdisciplinary approach in education.
Classification: LCC PE1404 .U74 2017 (print) |
LCC PE1404 (ebook) |
DDC 808/.0420711--dc23
LC record available at https://lccn.loc.gov/2016022685

13-digit ISBN: 978-1-62036-584-7 (cloth)
13-digit ISBN: 978-1-62036-585-4 (paperback)
13-digit ISBN: 978-1-62036-586-1 (library networkable e-edition)
13-digit ISBN: 978-1-62036-587-8 (consumer e-edition)

Printed in the United States of America

All first editions printed on acid-free paper
that meets the American National Standards Institute
Z39-48 Standard.

First Edition, 2017

We wish to thank Elon University and its Center for Engaged Learning for hosting the Critical Transitions: Writing and the Question of Transfer research seminar that prompted this collection. The "Transfer Camp" participants continue to enrich research and conversations about writing transfer in higher education. Finally, we remember Linda Bergmann (1950–2014) for the insight and humor she brought to the research seminar collaborations.

CONTENTS

PART TWO: PRINCIPLES AT WORK: IMPLICATIONS FOR PRACTICE
CASE STUDIES

Visit our companion website at www.understandingwritingtransfer.org for additional information.

FOREWORD

We congratulate Elon University for once again assuming a position of leadership in undergraduate education through its sponsorship of the Critical Transitions: Writing and the Question of Transfer research seminar. In this effort, Elon's Center for Engaged Learning facilitated international and multi-institutional research about writing transfer, and many of the findings from that research are recorded in this book.

We should confess to our readers that before we read this manuscript, even though we like to think we are up to speed with undergraduate education reform and improvement initiatives, we had never heard of writing transfer! So, for our continuing professional development and that of other readers, this book advances an important criterion for good writing: the ability to transfer one's writing skills to a variety of new contexts that exist in the present and will exist in the future.

There is no argument that writing is an essential skill for success not only in college but also in life beyond college. While virtually everyone will agree that good writing is important, that's where the consensus ends. The very definition of what it means to be a *good writer* differs across higher education stakeholder groups and the contexts for their work. The contributors argue that college and university faculty need to help students go beyond honing the writing skills learned in one setting and evaluated by a single instructor to understanding how to transfer those learned skills to multiple settings in which evaluation and expectations will be different, often vastly different from the usually abstract and somewhat artificial academic setting. The authors also argue that writing instruction should be far more than teaching correct spelling and sentence structure; rather, it should help students analyze the myriad "purposes, audiences, and contexts" for writing.

Scholarship on writing transfer is similar in some ways to the ideas behind "writing across the curriculum," but writing transfer goes further. The writers of this book acknowledge that writing must be transferred not only from course to course but also from high school to college, from general education to major disciplinary areas, from paper and pencil to technology, from a reliance on text messaging to writing in depth, and from college classrooms to a variety of work settings.

The starting point—the high school to college transition—is, of course, characterized by uneven levels of student preparation for the task of writing, and qualitative differences in the preparation and skills of those who teach writing at the pre-college level. There are significant differences in contemporary high schools in regard to the quality of instruction overall and what teachers expect and require from students. Therefore, when students move from high school to college, they are not on an even playing field in many areas, especially in regard to their abilities as writers. College and university faculty are often engaged in a sort of guessing game in terms of what their expectations should be, where to begin the process of writing instruction, and how to grade fairly. Topics such as writing transfer are likely to be put on the back burner in favor of giving students help with the most basic writing skills.

In our work with first-year college students and the faculty who teach them, we often encounter the expectation that writing in college is "once and done"—that the development of writing skills happens solely and appropriately in English 101. In fact, there are students who can negotiate a college or university curriculum in which writing is, truly, once and done in a single required first-year writing course or sequence. However, the problem does not belong only to students. There are faculty across disciplines who prefer to avoid student writing. Either they are uncomfortable with assigning and grading written work, or the number of students in their classrooms makes close attention to student essays or longer papers a virtual impossibility. This is further compounded by the reality that the dominant business model governing the delivery of the first-year curriculum is that of using adjunct professors who have neither the time nor financial incentive to read any more student writing than is absolutely necessary. If students take courses in which they are never or rarely required to write, their writing skills have no way of improving and, in fact, may actually decrease for lack of practice.

But the contributors of *Understanding Writing Transfer* argue for more than practice in writing clear sentences and paragraphs. They assert the importance of helping students learn to transfer writing skills to a variety of contexts. As educators who focus on the first year of higher education, we believe that a solid foundation for all aspects of writing begins in the first year, not only in the English 101/102 sequence but also in a well-crafted first-year seminar, which can be linked to another course in a learning community. First-year seminars, as well as many other high-impact practices, offer students the opportunity to learn more about writing and to practice low-stakes writing in a variety of forms—reflection papers, regular journal entries or letters to their instructors, and mini research papers.

Most first-year seminar instructors, who are either full-time or adjunct faculty and may not be skilled teachers of English, will benefit from faculty development that helps them to develop rubrics for providing feedback and/ or grading, understand and address common issues in first-year writing, and build familiarity with other campus writing experts and resources. The first-year seminar can also be an ideal setting for helping students to achieve a deeper understanding of purposes, audiences, and contexts for writing. Students can be given the opportunity to write for a technology platform, to hone their critical thinking skills through writing persuasive arguments or position papers, or to practice descriptive writing about the campus and its characters.

Understanding Writing Transfer can be an important tool in helping colleges and universities develop a clearer vision of their goals for student writing not only in the first year but also across the entire span of undergraduate education. While those goals may differ to some degree by institutional type, the book itself offers a template for any campus to use in cross-campus conversations about writing in the twenty-first century. These conversations could be designed to develop institution-wide goals for writing, to address issues of technology, to determine appropriate strategies for writing instruction for non-native English speakers, to expose campus employees to existing writing resources, and to explore the importance of connecting writing to high-impact practices such as undergraduate research, study abroad or away, learning communities, internships, and the first-year seminar. Cross-campus conversations can also be a site for sharing what works—the strategies instructors across disciplines are using to help students understand appropriate writing in specific disciplinary and professional contexts. This book offers a number of such strategies that can be valuable to readers.

We would like to leave you with the following questions:

1. After reading this book, how do you think your institution is performing at giving students the knowledge about and practice of writing transfer? Where and when does this occur?
2. How could your institution use this book to bring together stakeholders and writing experts to expand and improve efforts to develop students' abilities in writing transfer?

As your students "go forth," they will be forever judged professionally on the quality of their writing and their writing transfer abilities, and hence so will your college or university for whom each former student is an ambassador without—or perhaps literally with—a portfolio.

Betsy O. Barefoot, Senior Scholar, John N. Gardner Institute
John N. Gardner, President, John N. Gardner Institute

FIVE ESSENTIAL PRINCIPLES ABOUT WRITING TRANSFER

Jessie L. Moore

Writing curricula in higher education are constructed under a foundational premise that writing can be taught—and that writing knowledge can be "transferred" to new contexts. In the United States, first-year composition is often required for all students with the assumption that what is learned there will transfer across "critical transitions" to other course work, to postgraduation writing in new workplaces, or to writing in graduate or professional programs. Arguably, all of modern education is based on the broader assumption that what one learns *here* can transfer over *there*, across critical transitions. But what do we really know about transfer, in general, and writing transfer, in particular?

From 2011 to 2013, 45 writing researchers from 28 institutions in 5 countries participated in the Elon University's Critical Transitions: Writing and the Question of Transfer research seminar. As part of the seminar, Elon's Center for Engaged Learning facilitated international, multi-institutional research about writing transfer and fostered discussions about recognizing, identifying enabling practices for, and developing working principles about writing transfer. Over the final year of the seminar, participants developed the *Elon Statement on Writing Transfer* (2015) to summarize and synthesize the seminar's overarching discussion about writing and transfer, not as an end point but in an effort to provide a framework for *continued* inquiry and theory building (Anson & Moore, 2016). Although that document exists as a resource for disciplinary scholars in writing studies, this collection focuses on five essential principles about writing transfer that should inform decision-making by all higher education stakeholders. Part One: Critical Sites of Impact includes six chapters that examine programmatic and curricular sites that could be enriched by additional focus on these essential principles for writing transfer. Part Two: Principles at Work: Implications for Practice includes six case studies that illustrate the essential principles' implications for practice, curriculum design, and/or policy.

This collection concisely summarizes what we know about writing transfer and explores the implications of writing transfer research for universities' institutional decisions about writing across the curriculum requirements, general education programs, online and hybrid learning, outcomes assessment, writing-supported experiential learning, ePortfolios, first-year experiences, and other higher education initiatives. Ultimately, this brief volume aims to make writing transfer research accessible to administrators, faculty decision makers, and other stakeholders across the curriculum who have a vested interest in preparing students to succeed in their future writing tasks in academia, the workplace, and their civic lives.

What Is Writing Transfer?

Briefly, *writing transfer* refers to a writer's ability to repurpose or transform prior knowledge about writing for a new audience, purpose, and context. Writing transfer research builds on broader studies in educational psychology and related fields on transfer of learning, and many of the terms used to describe writing transfer are borrowed from these other realms. The following is a quick primer on some of the terms and concepts used in this collection.

David Perkins, a founding member of Harvard's Project Zero, and Gavriel Salomon, an educational psychologist, coined the two sets of terms often invoked in transfer studies, including writing transfer studies: *near transfer* and *far transfer*, and *high-road transfer* and *low-road transfer* (see Perkins & Salomon, 1988, 1989, 1992; Salomon & Perkins, 1989). Near transfer refers to carrying prior knowledge or skill across similar contexts (e.g., driving a truck after driving a car), whereas far transfer refers to carrying knowledge across different contexts that have little, if any, overlap (e.g., applying chess strategies to a political campaign). Whereas this first set of terms focuses on the contexts for transfer, the second set focuses on the learner's use of knowledge in those contexts. In low-road transfer, something is practiced in a variety of contexts until it becomes second nature and is automatically triggered when a new context calls on our use of the knowledge, skill, or strategy. High-road transfer, in contrast, requires the learner's mindful abstraction to identify relevant prior knowledge and apply it in the new context.

King Beach, a developmental psychologist, introduced the idea of *consequential transitions* as an alternate way to conceptualize use of prior knowledge. Beach (2003) suggested that transition refers to the generalization of knowledge across contexts. A consequential transition "is consciously reflected on, struggled with, and shifts the individual's sense of self or social position" (p. 42). Building on this concept, Terttu Tuomi-Gröhn and Yrjö Engeström (2003), from the Center for Research on Activity, Development and Learning, situated consequential transitions within activity systems, which shape and are shaped by learners and other participants. Successful transfer requires learners to implement new models based on their analyses of prior knowledge and to consolidate new and prior practices. Learners become boundary crossers and change agents, intertwined with evolving social contexts.

The Bioecological Model of Human Development, theorized by Urie Bronfenbrenner and colleagues, and Etienne Wenger's work on Communities of Practice help educators understand learners' interactions with those social contexts. The Bioecological Model attends to the context of learner development, extending the focus on the individual in the system to consider the impact of the individual's interactions with his or her context over time (see, e.g., Bronfenbrenner & Morris, 2006). Applied to transfer studies, the bioecological model suggests that the learner's dispositions can impact willingness to engage with transfer and can have generative or disruptive impacts on the learner's context. Similarly, Etienne Wenger and others suggested that communities of practice are collectives of individuals and groups sharing values, goals, and interests, with the community shaping the individual and the individual shaping the community (see, e.g., Wenger, McDermott, & Snyder, 2002). Communities include both novices and experts. Part of the dialogic process of moving from novice to expert involves learning how to learn within communities. As we think about learning transfer, then, we should look for the enabling practices that help students develop those learning-how-to-learn strategies that apply across contexts or communities.

Jan (Erik) Meyer and Ray Land (2006), building on David Perkins's notion of troublesome knowledge, challenged educators to identify concepts central to epistemological participation in disciplines and interdisciplines. Often these threshold concepts are transformative; when learners fully grasp the concepts, their disciplinary view changes. Yet, that transformative nature also creates liminality, as students grapple with ideas or new knowledge that may be counterintuitive or inconsistent with their prior knowledge. If students successfully work through the transitional space of making sense of the threshold concept, it likely will have an integrative impact, helping students synthesize other disciplinary knowledge and concepts. Threshold concepts typically are implicit markers of disciplinary knowledge, but once educators explicitly identify those threshold concepts that are central to meaning-making in their fields (i.e., their communities of practice), they can prioritize teaching these concepts, in turn increasing the likelihood that students will carry an understanding of these core concepts into future course work and contexts. Writing studies scholars Linda Adler-Kassner and Elizabeth Wardle (2015) have led efforts to identify the threshold concepts for writing, and the essential principles in this volume in essence reflect the threshold concepts for designing university curricula and teaching for writing transfer.

Successful Writing Transfer Requires Transforming Prior Knowledge

Principle 1: Successful writing transfer requires transforming or repurposing prior knowledge (even if only slightly) for a new context to adequately meet the expectations of new audiences and fulfill new purposes for writing. "Successful writing transfer occurs when a writer can transform rhetorical knowledge and rhetorical awareness into performance" (2015, p. 4). Students facing a new and difficult writing task draw on previous knowledge about genre conventions (e.g., reader expectations for memos or lab reports or patient reports), logical appeals, organization, citation conventions, and much more. They repurpose prior writing strategies, ranging from brainstorming activities to strategies for eliciting and responding to feedback on writing in progress. Whether crossing concurrent contexts (e.g., courses in the same semester, or university course work and a part-time job) or sequential contexts (e.g., courses in a major's or minor's scaffolded sequence, high school to college, or a university degree program to a postgraduation job), individuals may engage in both routinized (low-road) and transformative (high-road) forms of transfer as they draw on and use prior knowledge about writing.

When students tap that prior knowledge, they must transform or repurpose it, if only slightly. Writing studies scholars Mary Jo Reiff and Anis Bawarshi (2011), for instance, introduced the idea of "not-talk." They suggested that one part of repurposing prior knowledge is recognizing when a new task calls on writers to compose a genre that is *unlike* a genre composed before. In other words, successful transfer requires writers to recognize when the new task is not a five-paragraph essay, not a literary analysis, not a lab report, not a memo, and so forth.

Of course, genre knowledge is only one element of each rhetorical situation for writing. Successful writers also are attentive to the knowledge and expertise they bring to a writing task, the expectations and backgrounds of their readers, their available choices for the content and form of the actual text, and the larger context encompassing their communication. Being attentive to this rhetorical situation (as illustrated in Figure 1.1) enables

Figure 1.1. Elements of a rhetorical situation for writing.

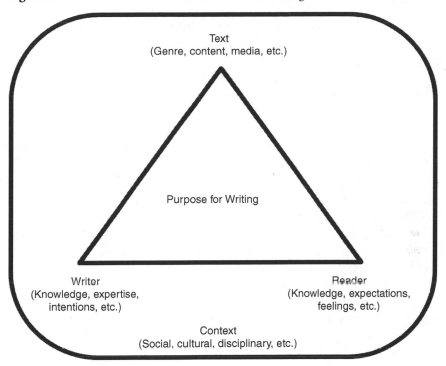

writers to make strategic choices about their prior knowledge that might be applicable—or adaptable—to each new purpose for writing.

Writing studies scholar Rebecca Nowacek (2011) highlighted the challenges inherent in transforming and repurposing writing knowledge for new rhetorical situations. Because students' transformation attempts typically are not visible to others, teachers often do not recognize those attempts. At the same time, the attempted transformation might not be appropriate for the new rhetorical situation, course, or writing context. Yet, if a teacher does not recognize that a student attempted to transfer prior knowledge, feedback to the student likely won't include strategies for more effective repurposing of that prior knowledge.

Given the significance of prior knowledge, higher education curricula must be attentive to the foundations laid in secondary curricula (see Farrell, Kane, Dube, & Salchak, this volume), in first-year courses (see Boyd, this volume; Gorzelsky, Hayes, Jones, & Driscoll, this volume; Robertson & Taczak, this volume), and in prerequisites throughout students' course work.

Writing Transfer Is a Complex Phenomenon

Principle 2: Writing transfer is a complex phenomenon and understanding that complexity is central to facilitating students' successful consequential transitions, whether among university writing tasks or between academic and workplace or civic contexts. Writing transfer is inherently complex. It involves approaching new and unfamiliar writing tasks through applying, remixing, or integrating previous knowledge, skills, strategies, and dispositions. If the new context does not trigger automatic use of prior knowledge, as in low-road transfer, writers must systematically reflect on past writing experiences that might be relevant, cull the prior knowledge that contributed to the success (or failure) of those past experiences, and adapt the knowledge for the new circumstances (high-road transfer).

Writing studies scholars Liane Robertson, Kara Taczak, and Kathleen Blake Yancey (2012) described the varied ways students use new writing knowledge relative to prior knowledge. Some students "take up new knowledge . . . by grafting isolated bits of new knowledge onto a continuing schema of the old," forming an assemblage, whereas other students revise and remix their prior knowledge to integrate new strategies and concepts, increasing the likelihood of success in their attempts to adapt and apply that cumulative, remixed knowledge to future writing tasks (Robertson et al., 2012).

In addition to the differences in how individual students assemble or remix prior knowledge, each new context for writing also provides affordances and constraints that impact that use of prior knowledge. Writing studies scholars Neil Baird and Bradley Dilger (in press), for example, highlighted how internship tasks and related mentoring can trigger—or fail to trigger—transfer and how students' dispositions compound the likelihood of success. Similarly, Nowacek (2011) reminded us that subsequent contexts for writing may not trigger students to reflect on relevant prior knowledge, both because the new context may be too different from the old context (cases necessitating far transfer) and because others in the new context (e.g., teachers, supervisors, etc.) may not offer prompts signaling that they expect the writer to draw on and adapt prior knowledge. Furthermore, reductive understandings of the complexity of writing transfer, like those found in the Common Core Standards, will hinder students' future writing transfer attempts by introducing false constraints (see Adler-Kassner, this volume).

Ultimately, writing transfer successes and challenges cannot be understood without exploring how individual learners are processing prior and new knowledge or without attention to learners' social–cultural spaces, including the standards and curricula that shape them. Adding to this complexity, stakeholders across university campuses often have different expectations for students' writing knowledge and practices (Werder, this volume).

Students' Identities Inform the Success of Their Writing Transfer Experiences

Principle 3: Students' dispositions (e.g., habits of mind) and identities inform the success of their unique writing transfer experiences. Writing transfer is not a discrete point along a student's educational path. Rather, writing transfer across critical transitions (e.g., from first-year writing to writing in the major or from writing in a capstone course to writing in the workplace) reflects one, in-flex moment in students' multidimensional lives. Everything else that forms students' identities—prior experiences, concurrent interests, values, beliefs, and so forth—continues to shape students' transfer attempts. Encapsulated in those identities are the dispositions or habits of mind that determine how learners use prior knowledge—whether, for instance, they will approach new knowledge as assemblage or remixing. Writing studies scholars Dana Driscoll and Jennifer Wells (2012) emphasized that dispositions can be generative or troublesome and context specific or generalizable. Some dispositions seem to better afford engaged rhetorical problem-solving. We are only starting to explore what such dispositions might be, so pedagogy that promotes transfer needs to be attentive to dispositions research.

Farrell, Kane, Dube, and Salchak (this volume), all participants in the Elon research seminar on Critical Transitions, examined students' critical transitions from high school to public and private universities in the United States, South Africa, and Ireland. Students at all three sites were optimistic about their ability to improve as writers, but they differed in their confidence in how well their high school courses had prepared them for university-level writing. Therefore, writing curricula must be attentive to individual identities—including confidence levels—as they teach for transfer.

University Programs Can "Teach for Transfer"

Principle 4: University programs (first-year writing programs, writing across the curriculum programs, majors, etc.) can "teach for transfer." Enabling practices that promote writing transfer include constructing writing curricula and classes that focus on the study and practice of rhetorically based concepts (e.g., genre, purpose, and audience) that prepare students to analyze expectations for writing and learning within specific contexts, asking students to engage in activities that foster the development of metacognitive awareness, and explicitly modeling transfer-focused thinking. First and foremost, writing programs should construct writing curricula and classes that focus on the study of and practice with writing knowledge. Learning rhetorically based concepts, such as genre, purpose, audience, and other elements of rhetorical situations, enables students to analyze expectations for writing and learning within and across specific contexts. With explicit rhetorical education, students are more likely to transform rhetorical awareness into writing performance (see, e.g., the cases by Boyd, this volume; Goldschmidt, this volume; Gorzelsky, Hayes, Jones, & Driscoll, this volume; Robertson & Taczak, this volume).

Second, writing programs should engage students in activities that foster the development of metacognitive awareness. Teaching students to ask good questions about writing situations and helping them develop learning and problem-solving strategies for analyzing unfamiliar writing situations will improve the likelihood of both low-road and high-road transfer. Both "teaching for transfer" (Robertson & Taczak, this volume; Yancey, Robertson, & Taczak, 2014) and "writing about writing" (Downs & Wardle, 2011, 2014; Gorzelsky et al., this volume) curricula forefront rhetorical knowledge, terms, and concepts that students will need to apply in future contexts. These approaches typically also build in reiterative opportunities for developing metacognitive awareness. As a result, they equip students with tools and strategies for successful boundary crossing.

Third, faculty across the curriculum should explicitly model transfer-focused thinking and the application of metacognitive awareness as a conscious and explicit part of learning. Although teaching for writing transfer curricula often are implemented in first-year writing contexts, courses university-wide can include reflection activities about both generalizable and discipline-specific writing strategies. Helping students develop strategies and tools to think about how writing functions in different rhetorical situations—and across different academic disciplines—prepares them to draw effectively on prior knowledge when they encounter writing in new settings, whether writing for a major, writing in a workplace, or writing for extracurricular activities.

Recognizing Writing Transfer Requires Mixed Methods

Principle 5: Recognizing and assessing writing transfer require using a mix of qualitative and quantitative methods looking at both critical transition points and longitudinal patterns of learning. Given the complexity of transfer, assessments of learning and research on writing transfer should use multiple methods to identify moments of transfer and to examine how writers repurpose their prior knowledge. As writing studies scholar Elizabeth Wardle (2007) noted, how you conceive of transfer will inform what you look for. As a result, university campuses must be attentive to misalignments in expectations (Werder, this volume) when they assess writing transfer.

Similarly, different methods will highlight different elements of the writer's activity system. Surveys and interviews may provide a glimpse of a writer's perception of his or her use of prior knowledge or a teacher's understanding of how a student might be repurposing writing skills and strategies. Textual or discourse analysis across time may show developing patterns of writing practices. Classroom observations may illustrate some affordances or constraints for a discrete writing task. In isolation, though, none of these research and assessment methods give us a complete picture of how curricula help students develop writing knowledge, when writing practices become routinized (for low-road transfer), and how students work through repurposing and transforming prior writing knowledge for new situations with new audiences and purposes (for high-road transfer). As Reiff and Bawarshi (2011) emphasized, understanding the complex boundary crossing that writers practice as they move among and write within varied activity systems requires using multiple methods.

Writing transfer studies, therefore, use a variety of qualitative and quantitative methods to identify evidence of and measure transfer, including surveys, focus groups, interviews, classroom observations, text analysis, discourse analysis, compose-aloud and think-aloud protocols, group discussion logs, and analysis of students' course work and faculty comments. Although students often are the primary participants in transfer studies, researchers also interact with and collect data from teachers and community partners. Most transfer studies are short term (one or two terms), but additional longitudinal studies and studies that examine both writers' academic and nonacademic activity systems are needed to extend higher education's understanding of writing transfer and to assess the effectiveness of writing-related curricula.

Many of the Principles at Work cases in this volume reiterate the value of using mixed methods across multiple contexts to achieve a scalable understanding of writing transfer—enabling teacher-scholars both to focus in detail on specific communities of practice and activity systems and to zoom out to examine working principles of writing transfer that apply across multiple contexts. For this reason, both short-term and longitudinal studies will enrich higher education's understandings of transfer, particularly as scholars examine learners' development as writers, not merely their transitions from one context to another. Adding student voices as participants, or even as coinquirers (e.g., Wardle & Clement, this volume), facilitates this more

TABLE 1.1
Chapters and Research Cases That Illustrate the Five Essential Principles

Essential Principle	Critical Sites of Impact	Principles at Work: Implications for Practice
1. Writing transfer requires transforming or repurposing prior knowledge.	Chapters 2, 3, 6, and 7	Chapters 8, 9, 11, 12, and 13
2. Writing transfer is a complex phenomenon.	Chapters 2, 3, 5, and 6	Chapter 13
3. Students' dispositions and identities inform their writing transfer experiences.	Chapters 3 and 6	Chapters 8 and 10
4. University programs can "teach for transfer."	Chapters 2, 3, 4, 5, and 6	Chapters 9, 10, 11, and 13
5. Recognizing and assessing writing transfer require multiple methods.	Chapters 4 and 7	Chapter 13

holistic examination of learners' development, boundary crossing, remixing, and integration.

Cross-institutional, cross-disciplinary, and cross-cultural collaboration enriches the discussion about writing transfer and allows new perspectives to become visible. Even if multi-institutional research is not feasible for a specific writing transfer study, testing the applicability of findings to other higher education contexts is crucial to understanding which curricular strategies for teaching for writing transfer are generalizable and which are context specific. Therefore, tenure and promotion systems should value these crucial efforts to replicate research across contexts.

The chapters and research cases that follow illustrate these five essential principles in more detail at critical sites of impact across higher education and explore their implications for practice, curriculum design, and higher education policies (see Table 1.1).

References

Adler-Kassner, L., & Wardle, E. (Eds.). (2015). *Naming what we know: Threshold concepts in writing studies.* Logan, UT: Utah State University Press.

Anson, C. M., & Moore, J. L. (Eds.). (2016). *Critical transitions: Writing and the question of transfer.* Fort Collins, CO: WAC Clearinghouse/University Press of Colorado.

Baird, N., & Dilger, B. (in press). How students perceive transitions: Dispositions and transfer in internships. *College Composition and Communication.*

Beach, K. (2003). Consequential transitions: A developmental view of knowledge propagation through social organizations. In T. Tuomi-Gröhn & Y. Engeström (Eds.), *Between school and work: New perspectives on transfer and boundary-crossing* (pp. 39–61). Bingley, UK: Emerald Group.

Bronfenbrenner, U., & Morris, P. A. (2006). The bioecological model of human development. In R. M. Lerner & W. Damon (Eds.), *Handbook of child psychology* (Vol. 1, pp. 793–898). New York, NY: Wiley.

Downs, D., & Wardle, E. (2011). *Writing about writing: A college reader.* Boston, MA: Bedford/St. Martin's.

Downs, D., & Wardle, E. (2014). *Writing about writing: A college reader* (2nd ed.). Boston, MA: Bedford/St. Martin's.

Driscoll, D. L., & Wells, J. (2012). Beyond knowledge and skills: Writing transfer and the role of student dispositions. *Composition Forum, 26.* Retrieved from http://compositionforum.com/issue/26/beyond-knowledge-skills.php

Elon Statement on Writing Transfer. (2015). Retrieved from www.centerforengaged learning.org/elon-statement-on-writing-transfer/

Meyer, J. H. F., & Land, R. (2006). Threshold concepts and troublesome knowledge: An introduction. In J. H. F. Meyer & R. Land (Eds.), *Overcoming barriers to student understanding: Threshold concepts and troublesome knowledge* (pp. 3–18). London, UK: Routledge.

Nowacek, R. S. (2011). *Agents of integration: Understanding transfer as a rhetorical act.* Carbondale and Edwardsville, IL: Southern Illinois University Press.

Perkins, D. N., & Salomon, G. (1988). Teaching for transfer. *Educational Leadership, 46*(1), 22–32.

Perkins, D. N., & Salomon, G. (1989). Are cognitive skills context-bound? *Educational Researcher, 18*(1), 16–25.

Perkins, D. N., & Salomon, G. (1992). Transfer of learning. In T. N. Postlethwaite & T. Husen (Eds.), *International encyclopedia of education* (2nd ed.). Oxford, UK: Pergamon Press. Retrieved from http://learnweb.harvard.edu/alps/thinking/docs/traencyn.htm

Reiff, M. J., & Bawarshi, A. (2011). Tracing discursive resources: How students use prior genre knowledge to negotiate new writing contexts in first-year composition. *Written Communication, 28*(3), 312–337.

Robertson, L., Taczak, K., & Yancey, K. B. (2012). Notes toward a theory of prior knowledge and its role in college composers' transfer of knowledge and practice. *Composition Forum, 26.* Retrieved from http://compositionforum.com/issue/26/prior-knowledge-transfer.php

Salomon, G., & Perkins, D. N. (1989). Rocky roads to transfer: Rethinking mechanisms of a neglected phenomenon. *Educational Psychologist, 24*(2), 113–142.

Tuomi-Gröhn, T., & Engeström, Y. (2003). *Conceptualizing transfer: From standard notions to developmental perspectives.* In T. Tuomi-Gröhn & Y. Engeström (Eds.), *Between school and work: New perspectives on transfer and boundary-crossing* (pp. 19–38). Bingley, UK: Emerald Group.

Wardle, E. (2007). Understanding "transfer" from FYC: Preliminary results from a longitudinal study. *Writing Program Administration, 31*(1–2), 65–85.

Wenger, E., McDermott, R., & Snyder, W. M. (2002). *Cultivating communities of practice: A guide to managing knowledge.* Boston, MA: Harvard Business School Press.

Yancey, K. B., Robertson, L., & Taczak, K. (2014). *Writing across contexts: Transfer, composition, and sites of writing.* Logan, UT: Utah State University Press.

PART ONE

CRITICAL SITES OF IMPACT

TRANSFER AND EDUCATIONAL REFORM IN THE TWENTY-FIRST CENTURY

College and Career Readiness and the Common Core Standards

Linda Adler-Kassner

To talk about transfer of students' learning across contexts—from high school to college or from college to work, for instance—is to participate in a discussion about the purpose of school that has ranged (and, in some instances, raged) for the past 150 years. The idea that school's purpose is to cultivate particular kinds of something—knowledge, skills, dispositions, beliefs, attitudes, orientations—in students is at the core of the American commitment to education (see, e.g., Dewey, 1916). The broad literature on transfer, then, is associated with a question emerging from this commitment: For what situations and experiences should students learn to be prepared, and how can that learning be cultivated across contexts: educational, civic, professional, and otherwise?

These questions are central to researchers and teachers in the field of writing studies, who explore how and by whom *good literacy* is defined and with what values and what implications. And because writing plays essential roles in processes associated with transfer, especially in school settings, writing studies researchers are especially interested in and concerned about questions associated with transfer of writing as part of our larger research and teaching foci.

Of course, writing studies researchers are not the only ones concerned with questions about writing and transfer. Writing, after all, is everyone's business—at least, everyone believes that writing is his or her business. Because writing is so ubiquitous—something that virtually every educated (and even noneducated) individual uses every day for a variety of purposes, something that is increasingly used to determine what people are seen to know or not know—the push to precisely explain and measure what students should know to produce "good writing" and how that should be taught is a subject for wide public discussion. Perhaps for this reason, it also is a feature of prominent educational reform efforts like the Common Core Standards (CCS; see corestandards.org), the subject of this analysis. The CCS, implemented in the 2014–2015 academic year in 43 states,[1] contain examples of what good writing is that will shape how writing is taught. The extent to which those definitions reflect what the literature on transfer shows about this process, especially related to writing, should be of considerable concern to anyone interested in questions about learning and transfer, especially as they concern writing. This chapter, then, examines the Common Core's writing standards through the lens of transfer research.

Transfer and Its Affordances: Examining the Map

Before we turn to an examination of the CCS, it is important to briefly review what the research literature tells us about how to foster students' knowledge and abilities associated with writing between contexts—in other words, how to create conditions for successful transfer or transformation of learning, especially transfer of writing knowledge and abilities. As chapter 1 reminds us, transfer occurs when "new and unfamiliar writing tasks [are approached] through the application, remixing, or integration of previous knowledge, skills, strategies, and dispositions" (p. 6, this volume). Transfer is successful when

> 'a writer can transform rhetorical knowledge and rhetorical awareness into performance' (Elon Statement, 2015, p. 4). Students facing a new and difficult writing task draw on previous knowledge about genre conventions (e.g., reader expectations for memos or lab reports or patient reports, etc.), logical appeals, organization, citation conventions, and much more. They repurpose prior writing strategies, ranging from brainstorming activities to strategies for eliciting and responding to feedback on writing in progress.

To develop these abilities and orientations toward writing, students must have opportunities to develop rhetorical knowledge—that is, to learn how to analyze purposes, audiences, and contexts for writing and to understand the relationships between expectations for writing and those purposes, audiences, and contexts as part of a *learning process*—to successfully develop abilities and dispositions that will lead to successful transfer.

The five essential principles also emphasize the critical role of metacognition in the development of rhetorical awareness. Writers must be able to reflect on and analyze their own activities to make conscious decisions as they move among and between different audiences, purposes, contexts, and expectations for writing. Without rhetorical knowledge and metacognitive abilities, writers tend to want to apply preconceived ideas about what writing is or should be rather than be rhetorically sensitive to their audience and thus miss meeting audience expectations (Reiff & Bawarshi, 2011; Sommers & Saltz, 2004).

Finally, the *Elon Statement on Writing Transfer*, the disciplinary research document underlying the essential principles shared in this collection, outlines several enabling practices to support the development of writing knowledge and abilities critical for transfer, including "constructing writing curricula and classes that focus on study of and practice with concepts that enable students to analyze expectations for writing and learning within specific contexts. These can include rhetorically-based concepts (such as genre, purpose, and audience)" and "asking students to engage in activities that foster the development of metacognitive awareness, including asking good questions about writing situations and developing heuristics for analyzing unfamiliar writing situations" (*Elon Statement on Writing Transfer*, 2015, p. 4).

Writing Transfer and College and Career Readiness: The Common Core Standards

What is known *about* transfer has particular relevance in contemporary discussions on education. As those discussions take place in public fora (e.g., newspaper articles, policy reports, or other documents that circulate among informed audiences outside of and beyond the academy), they suggest that schools are *not* enabling students to become the kinds of successful learners who can transfer knowledge successfully among two specific contexts: school and work. This is the fundamental argument associated with *college and career readiness*, a frame that has become so dominant in discussions of the purpose of education that to question it is anathema. Achieve, a policy institute instrumental in guiding the development of the college and career readiness frame and the reform agenda extending from it, says that *college and career readiness*

> means that a high school graduate has the knowledge and skills in English and mathematics necessary to qualify for and succeed in entry-level, credit-bearing postsecondary coursework without the need for remediation—or

put another way, a high school graduate has the English and math knowledge and skills needed to qualify for and succeed in the postsecondary job
training and/or education necessary for their chosen career (i.e., community college, university, technical/vocational program, apprenticeship, or
significant on-the-job training). (Achieve, n.d.)

Read in one way, the goals of this agenda as they are captured in this definition are laudable. They suggest that educators focus on elements associated
with learning and performance that apply across contexts: college entrance
(at all types of colleges, from two-year vocational schools to liberal arts colleges to research-intensive universities) and careers (from auto mechanic to
gardener, from secretary to pastry chef). And from a very abstract perspective, it is possible to identify "knowledge and skills" that individuals would
need to be successful across this enormous range of contexts and sites. But
the closer one gets to *actual* sites of practice, whether a particular kind of
college or a particular kind of job, the more clear the specific *elements* of that
site of practice become. Herein, then, lies one of the primary issues with the
college and career readiness agenda writ large: Even in a globalizing economy,
the on-the-ground specifics of schools, workplaces, and individual experiences have distinct elements and qualities. No class, no school experience,
can teach students to be successful in *all* of these contexts for practice—in
part because success in any context is predicated on a learner's ability to do
the hard work of identifying what *is* necessary for success in specific contexts.

A framework *for* learning, then, is critical for learners' success, because
they will invariably need to learn how to learn to be successful. In regard to
writing, this framework consists of learning to conduct analyses to address
some specific questions: What are the expectations for writing here? What
kinds of purposes does writing serve and for what audiences? Within those
purposes, what kinds of content are most effective, and what kinds of structures for writing are used to convey or bring readers into the experience of that
content? Consider, for instance, two different workplaces. At Expert Systems,
a technical communication firm, writers create documentation for a computer program that restaurateurs use to run their businesses. The program
does everything from managing the reservation system to calculating split
checks to inputting ingredients and menus for a given meal. At Local Seafood,
a nonprofit whose mission is to move seafood directly from the fisherman or
fisherwoman to consumers, the three-person staff writes (among other things)
material for the website describing (and selling) the fisher-to-consumer model,
letters to local farmers' markets asking for a spot to sell the product, recipes for
the fish that are distributed to consumers, flyers for fishing and food-related
events, and so on. Successful writing across these two workplaces, both of

which are food involved, looks very different. More than ever before, then, a framework for learning that includes the ability to analyze expectations for success and experience is critical for college and career readiness.

The CCS are the most visible representations of the college and career readiness agenda. The CCS contain specific standards for writing, as well as standards for "Literacy in History/Social Sciences, Science, and Technical Subjects." This analysis focuses only on the writing standards for grades K–12 because these standards are intended to support transfer between writing in high school, college, and work and are most closely related to the principles outlined in the *Elon Statement* (2015) and other research on writing and transfer.[2]

The writing standards, as all the major "standard" areas in the document, are rooted in "College and Career Readiness Anchor Standards," which are then broken out into specific grade-level standards. For the current purposes, a focus on the 10 anchor standards will illustrate the areas of divergence and consistency between what is known about educating writers for success and the CCS. The late Arthur Applebee (2013), distinguished professor at the University of Albany, State University of New York, and a member of both the review and validation panels for the English language arts standards, provided a preview of the analysis to come when he explained that the Standards "contain the residues of all of our professional disagreements about the teaching of [writing]. Whatever you consider most important . . . you can find it somewhere in the standards and its accompanying documentation. And so can those who disagree" (p. 26).

The primary point of divergence between the CCS's anchor standards for writing and the literature on transfer concerns the following: What do writers need to know to be successful in college? In their career? As participants in the increasingly global culture? In the Standards, the answer to this question is closely (though not exclusively) linked to the production of three types of texts (argument, informative/explanatory, and narrative) as well as the development of processes for writing and research.

The first three anchor standards, included in Table 2.1, list these types of writing as most critical for college and career readiness. An appendix elaborating on research to support the Standards asserts that "the Standards put particular emphasis on students' ability to write sound arguments on substantive topics and issues," because this ability is perceived as "critical to college and career readiness" (NGA Center/CCSSO, 2010b, p. 24). Although an asterisk and footnote indicate "these broad types of writing include many subgenres," the three types of writing outlined here are developed with increasing levels of specificity over the considerably more detailed grade-level standards that follow.

TABLE 2.1
Standards 1 Through 3: Text Types and Purposes

Students will:
1. "Write arguments to support claims in an analysis of substantive topics or texts, using valid reasoning and relevant and sufficient evidence."
2. "Write informative/explanatory texts to examine and convey complex ideas and information clearly and accurately through the effective selection, organization, and analysis of content."
3. "Write narratives to develop real or imagined experiences or events using effective technique, well chose details, and well-structured sequences" (NGA Center/CCSSO, 2010a, p. 18).

With this category, "Text Types and Purposes," the Standards answer questions that the research literature on writing and transfer attests should be at the center of successful writers' efforts: What kind of writing is used in this situation, what are the features or conventions of that writing, and what roles do these features play for the audience, purpose, and context for the writing? Their response—"argumentative writing, informative/explanatory writing, and narrative writing" (NGA Center/CCSSO, 2010b, p. 42)—reflects two myths about writing that directly contradict the research-based principles in the *Elon Statement*: that there is a sort of baseline "good writing" and that all other expectations for and types of writing are variations on this baseline, and that these types of writing (argument, informative/explanatory, and narrative) are always the same things and do not change based on contexts, purposes, and audiences for writing.

Even if one were to accept the idea that *argument* is defined as making a case in writing, a definition that is so broad as to be virtually meaningless, the reality is that there is no such thing as "an argument." Even in academic disciplines, arguments look different, and those disciplines' arguments look different from, say, an op-ed piece. What content is included, what evidence is considered appropriate and credible, and how that evidence is included varies considerably based on the context, audience, genre, and conventions (formal and informal rules) for writing. For instance, take a literary analysis (a type of argument) that draws on and extensively cites the concept of *reactualizing*, drawing on the work of Slovenian theorist Slavoj Zizec, who himself is reconceptualizing the work of earlier theorists such as Karl Hegel—an argument constructed with what might, in another context, be considered impenetrable vocabulary, inappropriately long sentences with multiple dependent clauses set apart by commas and dashes, lengthy paragraphs that include both theoretical concepts and extended quotes from literary texts that are the subject of the analysis; this is one type of argument constructed, in part, in sentences like this one (112 words of a 205-word paragraph, excluding this parenthetical explanation).

Compare it, say, to an op-ed. Short sentences, short paragraphs. Vocabulary more accessible to a general audience. Like the last three sentences, in fact. (A paragraph, to this point, of 24 words.) *Argument* is hardly just one thing.

There are additional issues here as well. Research on writing indicates that the more strongly writers believe that writing always takes place within or always extends from specific forms (e.g., argument, informative/explanatory, and narrative) and the more rigid the ideas they have about what those forms look like, the less able they are to understand that successful writing requires flexibility (e.g., Reiff & Bawarshi, 2011; Robertson, Taczak, & Yancey, 2012; Sommers & Saltz, 2004). Writers must analyze the expectations for writing within specific contexts and make appropriate decisions within those contexts.

The three anchor standards in the next category, "Production and Distribution of Writing" (summarized in Table 2.2), focus on writing activities. These include metacognitive strategies, which the research on writing and transfer (including the five essential principles) has shown to be important for writers' success. In this area, then, there is some overlap between the Standards and what is known from writing and transfer research. However, it is important to note that these activities are to be applied to the three modes outlined in standards 1 through 3, so there is a question about the extent to which writers would be able to separate them from the production of argument, informative/explanatory, and narrative writing.

Standard 4, which invokes the words "task, purpose, and audience," could be interpreted as prompting writers to analyze what is (and is not) appropriate for writing given specific purposes and audiences. But because the three text types described in standards 1 through 3 (argument, informative/explanatory, and narrative) are the only text types emphasized here, it is difficult to know how other types of writing might be invoked or used in response to this analysis. Standard 5, which focuses on writing processes, positions writing as an activity developed over time, which does reflect the extensive literature on writing development and writing processes (that is not explicitly related to transfer per se). And standard 6, which refers to technology as an affordance for

TABLE 2.2
Standards 4 Through 6: Production and Distribution of Writing

Students will:
4. "Produce clear and coherent writing in which the development, organization, and style are appropriate to task, purpose, and audience" (NGA Center/ CCSSO, 2010a, p. 18).
5. "Develop and strengthen writing as needed by planning, revising, editing, rewriting, or trying a new approach"(NGA Center/CCSSO, 2010a, p. 18).
6. "Use technology, including the Internet, to produce and publish writing" (NGA Center/CCSSO, 2010a, p. 18).

publication, also speaks to an important point from the literature on writing more broadly, and on transfer specifically, that students should write for real audiences. However, the extent to which that is possible given the dominance of the three texts types outlined in standards 1 through 3 is hard to know.

Anchor standards 7 through 9 (see Table 2.3) focus on "Research to Build and Present Knowledge." Although they revolve around the development of a question and the gathering, assessment, and use of sources to respond to that question, they fail to require that research be situated within a specific context. In fairness, this is an issue that also extends to some current instructional practices as teachers (in high school and college) continue to teach some version of a "research paper" that is entirely generic. Research-based writing, after all, is like all other writing: It is always created for a specific audience, a specific purpose, and a specific context. These standards, then, focus on research *processes* but do not situate research within specific contexts and purposes. This divergence from principles of transfer is especially consequential for activities like those mentioned in standard 8 related to gathering sources, assessing their credibility, and using them in writing. There is a complicated relationship between "credibility" and use of sources in specific contexts and genres. In other words, what is and is not credible and how "credible" sources are used "appropriately" is highly dependent on the context where the writing is produced, consumed, and distributed. This issue is also reflected in standard 9, which also refers to only the production of literary or informational texts, when there are many other types of sources that might constitute credible, valid, and important sources on which to draw for research-based writing depending on the context where the writing is situated. The tenth and last anchor standard, "Range of Writing," focuses on the habituated practice of writing "over extended time frames . . . and shorter time frames [for] a range of tasks, purposes, and audiences"(NGA Center/CCSSO, 2010a, p. 18). This standard also reflects writing as an activity and is consistent with best practices in writing instruction (e.g., National Council of Teachers of English [NCTE]).

TABLE 2.3
Standards 7 Through 9: Research to Build and Present Knowledge

Students will:
7. "Conduct short as well as more sustained research projects based on focused questions, demonstrating understanding of the subject" (NGA Center/ CCSSO, 2010a, p. 18).
8. "Gather relevant information from multiple print and digital sources, assess the credibility and accuracy of each source, and integrate the information while avoiding plagiarism" (NGA Center/CCSSO, 2010a, p. 18).
9. "Draw evidence from literary or informational texts to support analysis, reflection, and research" (NGA Center/CCSSO, 2010a, p. 18).

The areas of divergence between the Standards and the research on transfer are exacerbated when examination shifts from the anchor standards to the grade-level content standards. As Applebee noted, these "trivial[ize] both the [anchor] Standards and [the act and process of] writing and reflect an artificial, atomized model of writing development" (Applebee, 2013, pp. 28–29). A quick examination of standard 1b in Table 2.4, associated with writing arguments (as an elaboration of anchor standard 1, associated with the production of argument), illustrates the point. I italicized the differences between the standards as they are written from grade to grade.

As Applebee (2013) pointed out, the incremental developmental model reflected in the Standards does not reflect what we know about the recursive nature of "writing [and] language skills" (p. 28). The "breakdown" of the standards is, he said, "at best bizarre" (p. 28). Referring to standards related to "evidence," he said, "Nobody is going to wait until grade 9 to suggest that students select the best evidence to support their point, or wait until grade 8 to ask for 'several' pieces of evidence when more than one is available" (p. 28). He continued, "The point here is not simply that it is difficult to specify appropriate grade-level differences in this way, but that such specification can lead to a distortion of curriculum and instruction" (p. 29).

Despite what seem some important divergences between the literature on transfer and the Common Core's writing standards, several caveats here are important. First, this analysis extends from documents outlining the anchor standards alone and then only the writing standards, not materials focusing

TABLE 2.4
Standard 1b

Students will:
Grade 6: "Support claim(s) with clear reasons and relevant evidence, using credible sources and demonstrating an understanding of the topic or text" (NGA Center/CCSSO, 2010a, p. 42).
Grade 8: "Support claim(s) with *logical reasoning* and relevant evidence, using *accurate*, credible sources and demonstrating an understanding of the topic or text" (NGA Center/CCSSO, 2010a, p. 42).
Grades 9–10: "*Develop* claim(s) *and counterclaims fairly*, supplying evidence for each while *pointing out the strengths and limitations of both in a manner that anticipates the audience's knowledge level and concerns*" (NGA Center/CCSO, 2010a, p. 45).
Grades 11–12: "Develop claim(s) and counterclaims fairly and thoroughly, supplying the most relevant evidence for each while pointing out the strengths and limitations of both in a manner that anticipates *the audience's knowledge level, concerns, values, and possible biases*" (NGA Center/CCSO, 2010a, p. 45).

on implementation. Second, a number of professional organizations such as the National Writing Project and NCTE are working with teachers to develop materials that reflect research-based practices, including practices based on some research in transfer of learning. Third, elements of the ideas from this transfer research *are* reflected, to some extent, in the Standards, along with many other ideas. Fourth, it is up to individual districts (and, sometimes, schools) to decide how they want to deliver the Standards to students. Depending on the site, then, teachers may indeed create lessons and activities that reinforce the kind of flexibility and metacognitive awareness that the research indicates is critical for writers to successfully transfer or transform their practices from one site to another. But even some of these efforts come with notes of cautions, such as that sounded in a recent policy brief issued by NCTE (2013), "Implementation of the Common Core Standards." It warned of the "sometimes limited view of literacy in the CCSS [Common Core State Standards], the potential disconnect between CCSS and the understanding of literacy as socially and culturally situated, and the possibility that . . . forthcoming assessments will not support research-based instruction" (p. 3).

Conclusion: The Road to Transfer

In a recent article, education researchers David Perkins and Gavriel Salomon (2012) asserted that to transfer knowledge successfully, learners "have to build three mental bridges" (p. 250). Learners, they said, must "detect" possible links between what they learned in one situation and its possible application to another, "elect" to apply that knowledge, and "connect" the application of knowledge from one context to another to form a sort of generalizable principle that applies across situations.

Abundant research on writing, including that synthesized in the *Elon Statement*, tells us that successful writers are able to analyze purposes, audiences, and contexts where writing takes place; consider the role(s) that writing plays there; identify what they already know and what they need to know; and use all of this analysis to make conscious decisions about developing and shaping writing *for* those distinct purposes, audiences, and contexts. This is hardly a simple formula; instead, it requires developing a complex set of abilities and orientations toward writing and the role that writing plays within and across contexts. Any writer who approaches a writing task believing that "writing" involves simply replicating a form (e.g., an "argument" or a "narrative") and that that form will suffice in all situations is, as the research has shown repeatedly, not likely to be successful. To invoke Perkins and Salomon, writers taking this approach may "detect" the possibility for transfer, but what they "elect" to draw on will not likely help them to "connect" in appropriate ways from one learning context to the next.

This potential divergence between ideas about what is required for successful transfer is particularly consequential right now. The CCS are but one part of an educational reform agenda that is driving education policy in the United States. This agenda implies, in part, that there are generic skills and strategies that can lead to near-universal application. Yet, the research on transfer indicates that it is the ability to analyze the specific expectations among different contexts for practice, whether academic disciplines or workplaces, that contributes to writers' success. In the case of the CCS, it seems likely (especially in light of the assessments being developed to measure students' work with the Standards, a subject that space did not allow consideration of here) that students will experience writing as an increasingly constrained experience, something that is squeezed into three types of writing (argument, informative/explanatory, narrative) that are replicated in increasing specificity over 12 years of schooling.

The question that emerges from Perkins and Salomon's consideration of what is fostered (and not fostered) through these approaches, then, concerns the larger purposes of education—the same question, in fact, raised by Dewey (1916) 100 years ago and that has been asked consistently throughout the twentieth and twenty-first centuries: What should school be for, and what kinds of learning will help to achieve those purposes? In current efforts connected to the college and career readiness agenda, the answer is that school should prepare students for careers, but a narrowly defined notion of what that preparation is and should look like tends to run through efforts, like the CCSS, linked to that agenda. Perkins and Salomon (2012), instead, called for a "learning culture of opportunity" where learners "grope for potentially relevant prior knowledge (detect) and use judgment to decide on its relevance and how to proceed (elect). Such a culture . . . would not limit its activities strictly to the classroom, but reach beyond the walls" (p. 257). This broader view of learning points to a more complex idea of learning, one that research indicates good writers must experience to develop the abilities and orientations that research about transfer indicates are necessary for writers to become flexible.

Notes

1. This number, however, is in flux. During the drafting of this chapter alone, several states decided to drop the Standards and then chose again to use them.

2. Although U.S. Secretary of Education Arne Duncan (2012, 2013) likes to say that the Standards were developed by teachers within states and adopted voluntarily, critics of the Standards have repeatedly pointed out that this is not the case. Historian of education Diane Ravitch (2013) noted that the Standards were "developed by . . . Achieve and the National Governors association, both of which were generously funded by the Gates Foundation. There was minimal public engagement in the development of the Common Core. Their creation was neither grassroots nor did it emanate from the states" (see also Beers, 2009; Hicks, 2013).

References

Achieve. (n.d.). College and career readiness. Retrieved from www.achieve.org/college-and-career-readiness

Applebee, A. (2013). Common Core State Standards: The promise and the peril in a national palimpsest. *English Journal, 103*, 25–33.

Beers, K. (2009). An open letter about Common Core State Standards from NCTE President Kylene Beers. Retrieved from www.ncte.org/standards/common-core/response

Dewey, J. (1916). *Democracy and education.* New York, NY: Macmillan.

Duncan, A. (2012, February 16). *The Daily Show With Jon Stewart.* Retrieved from www.cc.com/video-clips/84qrrp/the-daily-show-with-jon-stewart-exclusive---arne-duncan-extended-interview-pt--1

Duncan, A. (2013, September 17). *The Colbert Report* [Season 9, Episode 09150].

Elon Statement on Writing Transfer. (2015). Retrieved from www.centerforengaged learning.org/elon-statement-on-writing-transfer/

Hicks, T. (2013). Tracing the Common Core in Michigan. Retrieved from http://hickstro.org/2013/09/30/tracing-the-common-core-in-michigan/

National Council of Teachers of English. (2013). Implementation of the Common Core Standards: A research brief produced by the National Council of Teachers of English. Retrieved from www.ncte.org/library/NCTEFiles/Resources/Journals/CC/0231-sep2013/CC0231Brief.pdf

National Governors Association Center for Best Practices and Council of Chief State School Officers (NGA Center/CCSSO). (2010a). *Common core state standards for English language arts & literacy in history/social studies, science, and technical subjects.* Retrieved from http://www.corestandards.org/wp-content/uploads/ELA_Standards1.pdf

National Governors Association Center for Best Practices and Council of Chief State School Officers (NGA Center/CCSSO). (2010b). Appendix A: Research supporting key elements of the standards. *Common core state standards for English language arts & literacy in history/social studies, science, and technical subjects.* Retrieved from http://www.corestandards.org/assets/Appendix_A.pdf

Perkins, D. N., & Salomon, G. (2012). Knowledge to go: A motivational and dispositional view of transfer. *Educational Psychologist, 47*(3), 248–258.

Ravitch, D. (2013, February 26). Why I cannot support the Common Core Standards [Blog]. Retrieved from https://dianeravitch.net/2013/02/26/why-i-cannot-support-the-common-core-standards/

Reiff, M. J., & Bawarshi, A. (2011). Tracing discursive resources: How students use prior genre knowledge to negotiate new writing contexts in first-year composition. *Written Communication, 28*, 312–337.

Robertson, L., Taczak, K., & Yancey, K. B. (2012). Notes toward a theory of prior knowledge and its role in college composers' transfer of knowledge and practice. *Composition Forum, 26.*

Sommers, N., & Saltz, L. (2004). Novice as expert: Writing the freshman year. *College Composition and Communication, 56*, 124–149.

3

PEDAGOGY AND LEARNING IN A DIGITAL ECOSYSTEM

Rebecca Frost Davis

Increasingly, learning happens beyond the boundaries of the physical classroom or even the virtual classroom of the learning management system as students and faculty create with digital tools and resources and interact with external, digital communities. What does transfer look like in this digital ecosystem? How easily do students make this transition? How might the principles of writing transfer outlined in chapter 1 inform pedagogy and learning in the digital ecosystem, and how can we best support successful transfer of learning into a digital ecosystem where graduates will increasingly pursue their personal, professional, and civic lives?

Learning in the Digital Ecosystem

To envision learning in the emerging digital ecosystem, consider the Century America Project ("About Century America," n.d.), a collaborative digital scholarship project linking history majors at 15 member institutions of the Council of Public Liberal Arts Colleges (COPLAC). In spring 2014 and spring 2015, Jeffrey McClurken of the University of Mary Washington and Ellen Holms Pearson of the University of North Carolina–Asheville led an intercampus course that produced the collaborative site. For class, students met twice weekly via video conference to talk about digital humanities tools and life in their school's town during the Great War and influenza outbreak. Students at each participating institution then built individual WordPress sites off the Century America domain to showcase primary sources collected from their institution and town, along with interactive maps and timelines (McClurken, 2016). For example, student Jennifer Marks (2014) at Truman

State University created the site "No Man's Land," for which she gathered, transcribed, and published online a collection of letters written by soldiers from Kirksville, Missouri, during and just after the war.

Such collaborative digital scholarship projects are powerful tools to link students to their communities and to see the application of their studies in community life. Students digitize resources and use primary historical data to fuel interpretation as they explore the authentic, ill-defined problem of how the Great War and influenza outbreak affected their local communities. This project combines at least three high-impact educational practices—undergraduate research, community-based learning, and capstone course and project—that have been demonstrated to increase student retention and engagement, thus leading to greater learning outcomes (Kuh, 2008). At the same time, this project engages multiple dimensions of what Randy Bass and Bret Eynon (2016) in *Open and Integrative: Designing Liberal Education for the New Digital Ecosystem* characterized as the emerging digital ecosystem: "The emerging ecosystem is shaped by networks, which are fundamentally social; characterized by horizontal access to creation and production; and increasingly driven by data, algorithms, and artificial intelligence" (p, 13). Digital networks enable the consortial network of COPLAC institutions to collaborate through video conferencing, a shared website, and other electronic communication tools. The Internet and intuitive digital publication tools like WordPress allow low-threshold open digital publication so that students can create and share knowledge and thus contribute to the historical narrative. Finally, by digitizing primary sources through both images and transcription, then creating interactive timelines and maps, students learn how data are created, structured, and analyzed with digital tools.

It is important to distinguish this emerging ecosystem as a site of transfer from the domain of online course delivery that replicates the circumscribed college-classroom in a digital context. Learning management systems maintain the boundaries of the classroom behind a log-in and add a variety of administrative tools for the instructor like the grade book, time-stamped assignment turn-in, quizzing, plagiarism detection, group management, announcements, and communication. The online discussion substitutes for in-class discussion. Lecture-capture technology allows the instructor to replicate the classroom lecture by combining recorded video of the instructor with slides. Although these tools have improved access to higher education and made instructors more productive, they do not focus on preparing students for the emerging digital ecosystem outside of a college's or university's control.

By contrast, consider how learning typically functions in the digital ecosystem. The popular video game Minecraft provides a good example. In

February 2014, *GameSpot* reported that Minecraft had passed 100 million registered users (Makuch, 2014). These players learn experientially by playing the game. They also create and share digital creations that extend the game through mods and skins, as well as YouTube videos of their game play, reviews of different mods, mash-ups of popular songs with Minecraft lyrics and videos, how-to videos, and so on. This community and its digital artifacts combine to exemplify what Henry Jenkins (2009) termed a *participatory culture*. Members create and share their creations across social networks. Learning happens by doing but also by informal mentorship from the most experienced to the novices (Jenkins, 2009, p. 3). Both danah boyd and Mimi Ito documented this learning phenomenon in youth culture, and, on the basis of this learning model, Ito and her colleagues called for the research and adoption of "connected learning" where students, driven by their own interests, connect to information and people for inquiry-guided learning (boyd, 2015; Ito, Okabe, & Tsuji, 2012). George Siemens's (2004) theory of connectivism is built on the same phenomenon of connected learning in the workplace. This type of learning thrives on the open networks, democratized knowledge production and creativity, and algorithms of the emerging digital ecosystem rather than the closed hierarchical environment of the learning management system.

Transfer in the Digital Ecosystem: Knowledge Construction

New digital tools and methodologies, the explosion of information, and low barriers to publication on the Internet have combined to make available to students myriad opportunities for authentic learning in the digital ecosystem (Lombardi, 2007). For example, online scholarly resources and projects enable students to join an academic community of practice in constructing and publishing knowledge online. The *Map of Early Modern London* (MoEML) began as a classroom tool for helping students understand Shakespeare's London and has evolved into an open-access, open peer review, open source, collaborative nexus of four related digital projects that provide cultural context for understanding Renaissance London aimed at both a scholarly and a more general audience (Jenstad, n.d.-a, n.d.-b). Through its Pedagogical Partnership program, MoEML allows instructors to act as guest editors for student contributions to the project (McLean-Fiander & Jenstad, n.d.).

By contributing to open digital projects like MoEML, students get to practice transferring their classroom learning to real-world, ill-defined problems. Lombardi (2007) explained the value of such authentic activities as a type of active learning that develops students in the conative domain where they are members of a disciplinary community and accountable for their work products. In particular, MoEML offers an opportunity for students to engage in the high-impact practice of undergraduate research. Blackwell and Martin (2009) argued for the necessity of this type of digital project that aims, at least in part, at a general public to engage students—especially in the humanities—in authentic scholarship aimed at nonprofessionals that parallels the value of student–faculty collaborative undergraduate research in the sciences. The low barriers to online publication have made opportunities like these abound, whether they are large-scale collaborative projects like MoEML, multi-institutional projects like the Century America Project, or the work of just one class, like the online books of local environmental history created by Michael Lewis's (2010) students.

On the surface, creating content for MoEML may seem like near transfer. Rather than writing an essay for the instructor, students in Shannon E. Kelley's Shakespeare class were instead assigned to "co-author an essay on an early modern London site of recreation" (Kelley, 2014). This assignment, however, requires that students recognize relevant prior learning and transform it in several ways (Principle 1). Rather than writing for the standards of a grade, students must write for the standards of the project, extensively defined through an editorial style guide, typographical conventions, and a checklist for submissions (Jenstad, n.d.-c). In this case, students cannot settle for a lower grade; their work must be revised until it meets these standards. Both the guidelines and the models of other entries give students important information about how they should transform their prior knowledge, but this is a complicated rhetorical shift. Students must first translate their writing knowledge to the disciplinary classroom and then to both an academic audience and the general public. They also are creating disciplinary knowledge as part of a larger project that extends in time both before and after the course and with which their work is in dialogue, evidenced through hyperlinks.

Conscious of the pedagogical challenges of teaching with this project and, no doubt, due to its pedagogical roots, MoEML provides extensive scaffolding that helps instructors teach for the transfer inherent in the project (Principle 4). These include an extensive welcome package; advice for students on research, writing for the web, and using disciplinary sources; and model syllabi and assignments. MoEML also supports assignments through interaction with the class in the form of a syllabus blurb about the project, a class visit via Skype, editorial review of an early draft, and templates and instructions for encoding according to Text Encoding Initiative (TEI) guidelines (McLean-Fiander & Jenstad, n.d.). Such resources and support provide useful models for instructors who may want to explore contributing to other digital projects that have not created such well-developed teaching supports.

MoEML also frames this experience as a professional scholarly activity by crediting the students on the website as contributors and the instructor as guest editor. This framing makes the experience of contribution more of an authentic scholarly work experience rather than yet another essay for an English class. Students gain insight into the professional standards and iterative process for knowledge creation that separates this vetted resource from other information on the web. This professional framing may also help make the experience of this assignment a consequential transition for students, as they take on the identity of working adult.

As this example of professionalization shows, attention should be paid to the complexity (Principle 2) of contributing to a project like MoEML and how this experience may affect a student's identity (Principle 3). First of all, it empowers students to create new knowledge. By publishing scholarly content online, students are helping create what Ed Ayers (2013) termed "*generative scholarship*—scholarship that builds ongoing, ever-growing digital environments even as it is used" (emphasis added). That is, they are creating resources that can be used to create more scholarship. Such creation may lead to a sense of efficacy or agency. Some digital projects have built in this sense of empowerment. For example, the mission of the History Harvest project is to change the dominant historical narrative by "harvesting" the history of underrepresented communities ("The History Harvest," n.d.). Other projects seek to effect change by democratizing access to information, such as the White Violence, Black Resistance project, cocreated by Toniesha Taylor and Amy E. Earhart (n.d.), which digitizes primary historical documents related to interactions of race and power that may be inaccessible to the local communities that produced them. They explained, "Our ongoing projects present an activist model grounded in the classroom where undergraduate students are participants in canon expansion while learning valuable research and digital literacy skills." In all of these examples, students experience the power of their academic work to effect change, an experience that may lead to a consequential transition for their identity. In 2015, the Association of American Colleges & Universities issued the LEAP challenge, which calls for all students to produce signature work—substantial projects or experiences driven by personal inquiry (Association of American Colleges & Universities, 2015). Projects like Century America represent such consequential signature work in the digital ecosystem.

Transfer in the Digital Ecosystem: Networks

The projects discussed in the previous section represent near transfer because they remain within the academic community. The digital ecosystem, however, also offers opportunities for students to interact with a variety of different net-worked communities that may require far transfer. The FemTechNet (femi-nist + technology + network) collective has created a pedagogical project that connects nodal courses in feminism and technology at all types of institutions in a larger network spanning across the United States and into Canada and the United Kingdom. This distributed online collaborative course (DOCC) is a "feminist retooling of the popular genre of networked learning called MOOCs (Massive Open Online Courses)" ("What Is a DOCC?" 2016), reflecting the origin of much digital pedagogy in opposition to dominant modes of online learning. Students interact with their classmates, peers at other campuses, and the larger FemTechNet "network of scholars, artists, and students working on, with, and at the borders of technology, science, and feminism" ("Network," 2016).

Beyond this academic network, students are encouraged to engage in networked communities in the digital ecosystem through digital tools that leverage the power of networks for collective action. For example, students at multiple campuses have taken part in the wiki-storming assignment to add feminist scholarship to already existing content on Wikipedia in conjunction with WikiProject Feminism (2016). By participating in Wikipedia's processes, students learned not only how to edit Wikipedia but also how to make their edits stick. Students must learn to work within the conventions of the Wikipedia community, such as the requirement for well-cited summaries of secondary sources rather than original content, explanation and justification of edits on the "Talk" page of an article, and labor (copyediting, grammatical corrections, etc.) for the community on other entries (Koh & Risam, 2013). In other words, this activity is community-engaged learning in a virtual community. This assignment exemplifies the power of digital networks to move classroom interaction beyond the instructor and classmates to peers at other campuses and to online communities, like the participatory culture of both WikiProject Feminism and the larger community of Wikipedia editors.

The wiki-storming assignment activates multiple principles of transfer. Students must transform prior knowledge (Principle 1) not only by paying attention to the rhetorical situation of the Wikipedia entry but also by con-sidering their rhetoric for two audiences: the general reader of Wikipedia and the community of Wikipedia editors. Effective edits require sustained engagement with the Wikipedia community so students must perform their writing process online, saving multiple drafts and explicitly reflecting on them by explaining their revisions on the "Talk" page. Essentially, students are transferring both their content knowledge and their metacognitive knowl-edge to the Wikipedia setting. Although access to such online communities is open, participation and effective engagement in the community depends on ongoing participation in the community's norms. The wiki-storming assignment helps students practice a skill that they will likely transfer and exercise in a variety of digitally networked communities throughout their life.

Developing the skills for this two-tier interaction (knowledge production and metacognitive reflection on knowledge production) requires intentional pedagogy (Principle 4). For this reason, the Wikimedia Foundation (2015) offered the model of "A 12-Week Assignment to Write a Wikipedia Article." Veteran Wikipedia editor and educator Adrianne Wadewitz interviewed by Elizabeth Losh in 2013 advised,

> "Not taking enough time to design an assignment" could be a fatal error committed by novices, particularly those who are excited by the potential for participatory learning. Diving right in and learning by trial and error "works for a lot of technology," but "with Wikipedia you are engaging with a lot of people on the other end," so you need to articulate feasible learning goals that respect existing community practices.

Although older forms of knowledge production enforce professional creation through gatekeeping, Wikipedia is deceptively open. At the same time, creators must participate in the conventions of the community to preserve their creation. These norms of behavior are not as obvious to outsiders; as an experienced member of the community, Wadewitz (Losh, 2013) offered mentoring to novices in a typical process of the participatory community. Instructors, then, are faced with the challenge of both learning new modes of creation themselves and helping students learn so that they develop agency to effect change in these environments. This challenge calls into question an instructor's authority based on content expertise signified by the terminal degree. Instead, instructors must adopt student-centered learning pedagogies and set scaffolded learning goals such as learning how to approach new networked communities, learning the conventions of participation, and creating new content and effecting change through that creation by shifting the male-centric perspective of Wikipedia. This complex set of learning goals, then, requires 12 weeks rather than the sort of one-off assignment to summarize content on a topic that one might expect.

Such a complex skill also depends on a student developing the confidence that she can effect change in a networked community, which in turn depends on student identity and attitude toward transfer (Principle 3). Notions of the digital native create pitfalls for student work in the digital ecosystem because of the complex nature of transfer (Bennett, Maton, & Kervin, 2008). On one hand, instructors might expect that students who routinely engage in online activity would be tech savvy and thus able to easily and successfully complete the wiki-storming activity. Indeed, on one hand, students with past experiences in online communities like those studied by danah boyd might be comfortable in negotiating the norms of a new networked community. On the other hand, however, they may not be comfortable with this new content area, which may hinder them from seeing the potential to transfer the skills of community participation that worked for them in another online community. Also, many students who are comfortable with intuitive interfaces are not confident in new academic content areas. Instructor expectations of student technology comfort might paradoxically undermine a student's confidence in this arena.

Transfer in the Digital Ecosystem: Change

So far I have focused on individual expeditions into the digital ecosystem that occur in the context of one class. Now, I turn to the larger implications of transferring learning into the emerging digital ecosystem for higher education curricula and institutions. What is the experience of students who encounter the digital ecosystem in multiple classes or students who have never encountered it in a class before? What has their prior learning been? How will skills developed working on MoEML transfer to wiki-storming? The first assignment aims to contribute to a digital resource, whereas the second has an explicit activist goal of changing that resource. And although both of these projects involved creating encyclopedia entries, there are many other digital projects and tools that offer a higher road to transfer, such as network analysis or text mining or computational chemistry. Students must develop resilience to deal with such technology change.

To help students develop resilience, instructors should explicitly address the digital ecosystem and model transfer-minded thinking. At Bryn Mawr College, Katherine Rowe invited her students to examine Facebook with the same critical eye they turned on items in their school archives (Davis, 2010). One of those students, Jen Rajchel (2010), went on to lobby for permission before creating the first online thesis in Bryn Mawr's English department, *Mooring Gaps: Marianne Moore's Bryn Mawr Poetry*. Rajchel traced her interest in digital scholarship to Rowe's class. Being transfer minded in a digital context means explicitly modeling the transfer of academic skills to the digital ecosystem and teaching students how to understand and critique their digital tools. Rajchel's persistence in completing a digital thesis is evidence of both her digital skills and her resilience.

Just as instructors need to teach for transfer (Principle 4), institutions of higher education likewise should scaffold the use of digital tools and resources across the curriculum, intentionally developing the skills and mind-set needed for lifelong learning in the digital ecosystem. For example, a first-year seminar on literature might use social annotation with tools like

Hypothes.is to surface reading practices and encourage dialog around a text (Dean, 2015). A science class might encourage students to contribute to a citizen-science project by capturing data using the iNaturalist App (Davis, 2014). Other science students might explore the possibility of life on other planets using the Habitable Worlds simulation ("Habworlds Beyond," n.d.), while German students build fake German identities in a virtual world called Pfefferhausen (http://pfefferhausen.weebly.com) created using the website tool Weebly, and political science students create peace in the Middle East using the game Peacemaker (www.peacemakergame.com). Some of these experiences occur within physical or virtual classrooms, whereas others occur in the digital ecosystem. This repeated and varied experience should prepare students well for the technological change they are likely to face in their lifetimes by effecting a consequential transition into a mind-set of resilience (Principles 2 and 3). To create a curriculum that effectively integrates the digital ecosystem, faculty are required to have significant development to learn digital tools and methods. If every department pursues this integration, however, students will experience transfer as they move through the curriculum without instructors having to learn multiple new tools. Instead, they can focus on the tool that works best for their own course.

Universities should also consider the implications of transfer as they design their technology environments. Rather than focusing on one closed learning platform, information technology departments should consider creating an ecosystem of learning technologies that facilitate transfer across the ecosystem and beyond. For example, the Learning Tools Interoperability specification lays the groundwork for standard integration between different learning tools ("Learning Tools Interoperability," n.d.) so that a learning management system like Blackboard or Canvas might allow integration with a collaborative writing tool like Google Docs. These technology ecosystems and university technology policies should enable instructors to move learning into the digital ecosystem beyond what is controlled by the institution so that students are ready to act in this environment when they graduate. Instructional technologists should be ready to advise faculty about the pros and cons of such open digital work, the implications for the Family Educational Rights and Privacy Act (FERPA), and the need to allow some students to perform alternate assignments (Smith, 2012). Instructional designers, department chairs, and others should encourage instructors to move technology use to the higher levels of Ruben Puentedura's (2014) Substitution Augmentation Modification Redefinition model by focusing on tasks that are significantly redesigned because of technology or even impossible without technology rather than simply replacing analog with digital with no functional change.

Conclusion: Pedagogy of Transfer in the Digital Ecosystem

Considering the principles of writing transfer in the context of the digital ecosystem points us to important considerations for all instructors as they face the challenge of empowering students to transfer their academic learning to a digital context. Digital projects, networks, communities, and resources provide ample opportunities for students to transfer their learning—near or far, high road or low road (Principle 1). The authentic, unscripted problems; networked communities; and real-world experiences may lead to consequential transitions for students moving into adulthood (Principle 2). In particular, technological change requires a resilient mind-set (Principle 3). In the face of these complex situations, teaching for transfer becomes all the more important (Principle 4). Projects like MoEML and Wikipedia provide important models for this teaching, but many digital projects and environments offer no such pedagogical support. Because the digital ecosystem is constantly evolving, instructors, too, must practice transfer by adopting effective pedagogical structures from one project to another. Fortunately, most instructors are good at transfer; they just need the models to inspire their own new assignments and teaching ideas. A participatory culture of digital pedagogy has evolved in the open digital ecosystem that shares such models, including Humanities, Arts, Science, and Technology Alliance and Collaboratory (HASTAC, n.d.) and The Pedagogy Project (Barnett, 2014); *Digital Pedagogy in the Humanities: Concepts, Models, and Experiments* (Davis, Gold, Harris, & Sayers, 2016); the Science Education Resource Center at Carleton College (http://serc.carleton.edu/index.html); *Hybrid Pedagogy*; and the *Journal of Interactive Technology and Pedagogy*, to name just a few. The next step in developing this digital pedagogy is to transfer the methodologies that have been developed for recognizing and studying writing transfer (Principle 5) and use them to analyze transfer in the digital ecosystem.

References

About Century America. (n.d.). Retrieved February 25, 2016, from http://centuryamerica.org/about/

Association of American Colleges & Universities. (2015). The LEAP challenge: Education for a world of unscripted problems. Retrieved from www.aacu.org/sites/default/files/files/LEAP/LEAPChallengeBrochure.pdf

Ayers, E. L. (2013). Does digital scholarship have a future? *EDUCAUSE Review, 48*(4). Retrieved from http://er.educause.edu/articles/2013/8/does-digital-scholarship-have-a-future

Barnett, F. (2014, April 1). The Pedagogy Project. Retrieved from www.hastac.org/pedagogy-project

Bass, R., & Eynon, B. (2016). *Open and integrative: Designing liberal education for the new digital ecosystem.* Washington, DC: Association of American Colleges & Universities.

Bennett, S., Maton, K., & Kervin, L. (2008). The "digital natives" debate: A critical review of the evidence. *British Journal of Educational Technology, 39*(5), 775–786. Retrieved rom http://doi.org/10.1111/j.1467-8535.2007.00793.x

Blackwell, C., & Martin, T. R. (2009). Technology, collaboration, and undergraduate research. *Digital Humanities Quarterly, 3*(1). Retrieved from www.digitalhumanities.org/dhq/vol/3/1/000024/000024.html

boyd, d. (2015). *It's complicated: The social lives of networked teens.* New Haven, CT: Yale University Press.

Davis, R. (2010, December 1). Learning from an undergraduate digital humanities project. Retrieved from http://blogs.nitle.org/2010/12/01/learning-from-an-undergraduate-digital-humanities-project/

Davis, R. F. (2014, March 18). Experiential learning at Wild Basin. Retrieved from http://sites.stedwards.edu/instructionaltechnology/2014/03/18/experiential-learning-at-wild-basin/

Davis, R. F., Gold, M. K., Harris, K. D., & Sayers, J. (Eds.). (2016). Digital pedagogy in the humanities: Concepts, models, and experiments. Retrieved from https://github.com/curateteaching/digitalpedagogy

Dean, J. (2015, August 25). Back to school with annotation: 10 ways to annotate with students; hypothesis. Retrieved from https://hypothes.is/blog/back-to-school-with-annotation-10-ways-to-annotate-with-students/

Feminist wiki-storming. (2016). Retrieved from http://femtechnet.org/docc/feminist-wiki-storming/

FemTechNet. (n.d.). Wikistorming. Retrieved from http://femtechnet.newschool.edu/wikistorming/

Habworlds Beyond. (n.d.). Retrieved February 25, 2016, from www.habworlds.org/

HASTAC: Changing the Way We Teach and Learn. (n.d.). Retrieved from www.hastac.org/node

Ito, M., Okabe, D., & Tsuji, I. (Eds.). (2012). *Fandom unbound: Otaku culture in a connected world.* New Haven, CT: Yale University Press.

Jenkins, H. (2009). *Confronting the challenges of participatory culture: Media education for the 21st century.* Cambridge, MA: MIT Press.

Jenstad, J. (n.d.-a). About MoEML. In J. Jenstad (Ed.), *The map of early modern London.* Retrieved from http://mapoflondon.uvic.ca/about.htm

Jenstad, J. (n.d.-b). History of MoEML. In J. Jenstad (Ed.), *The map of early modern London.* Retrieved from https://mapoflondon.uvic.ca/history.htm

Jenstad, J. (Ed.). (n.d.-c). Teaching with MoEML. In *The map of early modern London.* Retrieved from https://mapoflondon.uvic.ca/teaching.htm

Kelley, S. E. (2014, Fall). Syllabus, EN 213: Shakespeare I. Retrieved from https://mapoflondon.uvic.ca/docs/engl213_fall_2014_kelley.pdf

Koh, A., & Roopika, R. (2013). How to create Wikipedia entries that will stick. Retrieved from http://dhpoco.org/rewriting-wikipedia/how-to-create-wikipedia-entries-that-will-stick/

Kuh, G. D. (2008). *High-impact educational practices: What they are, who has access to them, and why they matter.* Washington, DC: Association of American Colleges & Universities. Retrieved from www.aacu.org/leap/hips

Learning tools interoperability. (n.d.). Retrieved from www.imsglobal.org/activity/learning-tools-interoperability

Lewis, M. (2010). In and out of the field. *Journal of Urban History, 36*(1), 68–80.

Lombardi, M. M. (2007). *Authentic learning for the 21st century: An overview* (ELI White Papers). Educause Learning Initiative. Retrieved from www.educause.edu/library/resources/authentic-learning-21st-century-overview

Losh, E. (2013, May 6). How to use Wikipedia as a teaching tool: Adrianne Wadewitz. Retrieved February 15, 2016, from http://dmlcentral.net/how-to-use-wikipedia-as-a-teaching-tool-adrianne-wadewitz/

Makuch, E. (2014, February 26). Minecraft passes 100 million registered users, 14.3 million sales on PC. *GameSpot.* Retrieved from www.gamespot.com/articles/minecraft-passes-100-million-registered-users-14-3-million-sales-on-pc/1100-6417972/

Marks, J. (2014). *About the project.* Retrieved from http://truman.centuryamerica.org/

McClurken, J. (2016, January 20). *Public.* Retrieved from https://github.com/curateteaching/digitalpedagogy

McLean-Fiander, K., & Jenstad, J. (n.d.). Pedagogical partners' welcome package. In J. Jenstad (Ed.), *The map of early modern London.* Retrieved from https://mapoflondon.uvic.ca/ppp_welcome.htm

Network. (2016). Retrieved from http://femtechnet.org/about/the-network/

Puentedura, R. (2014, September 24). SAMR and Bloom's taxonomy: Assembling the puzzle. Retrieved from www.graphite.org/blog/samr-and-blooms-taxonomy-assembling-the-puzzle

Rajchel, J. (2010). *Mooring gaps: Marianne Moore's Bryn Mawr poetry.* Bryn Mawr College. Retrieved from http://mooreandpoetry.blogs.brynmawr.edu/

Siemens, G. (2004, December 12). Connectivism: A learning theory for the digital age. Retrieved from http://devrijeruimte.org/content/artikelen/Connectivism.pdf

Smith, K. (2012, November 30). Guidelines for public, student class blogs: Ethics, legalities, FERPA and more. Retrieved from www.hastac.org/blogs/cathy-davidson/2012/11/30/guidelines-public-student-class-blogs-ethics-legalities-ferpa-and-mo

Taylor, T., & Earhart, A. E. (n.d.). White violence, Black resistance. Retrieved February 23, 2016, from https://sites.google.com/site/bkresist/

The History Harvest. (n.d.). Retrieved from http://historyharvest.unl.edu/about

What is a DOCC? (2016). Retrieved from http://femtechnet.org/docc/

Wikimedia Foundation. (2015). A 12-week assignment to write a Wikipedia article. Retrieved from http://outreach.wikimedia.org/wiki/Education/Syllabi

WikiProject Feminism. (2016, January 22). In *Wikipedia: The free encyclopedia.* Retrieved from https://en.wikipedia.org/w/index.php?title=Wikipedia:WikiProject_Feminism&oldid=701042256

4

WRITING, TRANSFER, AND ePORTFOLIOS

A Possible Trifecta in Supporting Student Learning

Kathleen Blake Yancey

Alarmed by what she perceived as deficiencies in U.S. higher education, Secretary of Education Margaret Spellings created the so-called Spellings Commission in 2006. Its purpose was to combine the four *A*s of postsecondary education—access, affordability, accountability, and assessment—to create a lens for inquiry into the U.S. educational system, all with an eye toward making its processes more transparent, its costs more affordable, and its results more clearly communicated to the public. Since that time, higher education, especially public higher education, has adopted a system of mechanisms, chief among them the Voluntary System of Accountability (VSA), intended to meet the standards established by the commission.

Despite these new efforts and their initialisms, however, one goal dominates all the activity intending to enhance the efficacy of higher education: increasing the graduation rates of students at both community colleges and four-year schools. Toward that end, we've seen several efforts, the most interesting of which combine research and recommendations. A perfect example of one such two-pronged effort is provided through the National Survey of Student Engagement (NSSE) and Community College Survey of Student Engagement (CCSSE) projects collecting data on high-impact practices. Those data and the contexts through which they can be interpreted provide multiple kinds of information that institutions can use to enhance practice and support students. Chief among these high-impact practices is instruction in writing, preferably on a consistent, programmatic basis, facilitating the learning of students throughout the life span of their college careers: at the entry point into college; as a site in general education; at the transition into and within the major, where writing functions as both the introduction to the major and the mechanism to secure the disciplinary knowledge of the major; and in service-learning and other cocurricular sites as a counterpart and complement to institutional curricula. All of these sites contribute to students' transitions into the post-university life of workplace and professional and graduate schools.

As students move across these sites during both the horizontal experience of general education and the vertical progression of the major, they "transfer" knowledge and practice in writing; that is, they take what they have learned—about writing itself and about how to write—in one setting and adapt it—appropriately, we hope—for another. In the words of the *Elon Statement on Writing Transfer* (2015),

> Successful writing transfer occurs when a writer can transform rhetorical knowledge and rhetorical awareness into performance. Students facing a new and difficult rhetorical task draw on previous knowledge and strategies, and when they do that, they must transform or repurpose that prior knowledge, if only slightly. (p. 4)

More specifically, we know from research into high-impact practices that students who write more often and receive responses to writing are more engaged in college, and we know that more engaged students stay in college longer and are more likely to graduate. We know from research on the transfer of knowledge and practice—in psychology, in learning theory, and in writing studies—that writing curricula, including reflective activities, can be designed to support such transfer across the college years. As this chapter explains, it's also the case that the sites of writing where students compose are, too often, balkanized, separated one from the next into general education classes too often disconnected from the major, classes in the major too often disconnected from extracurriculars, and both disconnected from future endeavors, be they in the workplace or in school.[1] A good question, then, is whether there is a kind of cross-curricular institutional space or structure that could provide an explicit opportunity for students to think about how they are transferring writing across these sites of composing, a space where students might document and comment on their writing development and in the process create their own theory of composing (Yancey, Robertson, & Taczak, 2014). One such site, possibly the most promising to date, is the electronic portfolio (ePortfolios)—a site where students collect, select, and reflect on their work and that has a successful track record of engaging students (Eynon, 2009; Yancey, 2009). Toward outlining this option, this chapter takes up the following tasks: (a) considering what transfer of writing knowledge and practice means in the context of writing across the college years; (b) defining more fully ePortfolios, paying specific attention to the central role of reflection in them and exploring the role that they might play in facilitating students' transfer of writing knowledge and practice; and (c) considering how and why educational policy might in turn want to employ the development of ePortfolios as a site for supporting such transfer.

Writing Across the College Years

Research into writing across the college years is relatively young. Universities began including writing in the first year of college in the late nineteenth century, but it wasn't until the 1970s that writing across the curriculum programs began. During the earlier (and greater) part of the twentieth century, writing was assigned in U.S. colleges and universities but not in any systematic or programmatic way. As important, the field of writing studies—which takes as one focus research into writing development and ways to support students, through both curriculum and pedagogy, as they progress through school—is also a later twentieth-century phenomenon, with some marking its origins at 1949 and others in the 1960s. Moreover, even though the two areas of inquiry—How do we support writers composing across the curriculum? How do we support entering college writers?—were seen as related, it's only recently that we have begun (a) thinking of them together, somewhat like two sides of the same coin, and (b) researching that relationship: How can we support entering college writers, and what are the best interfaces between a program focused on these writers and one supporting writers in the disciplinary majors?

Before we consider this second question, it's useful to briefly review the history of what has been taught in both contexts in the past 40 years, precisely because the research has shown that we can, in the words of cognitive psychologists David Perkins and Gavriel Salomon (1992), "teach for transfer." The one practice that has been consistently taught in college classes during this time is writing process, and if we can in fact teach for transfer, students should be transferring process; as explained later, they do. Put another way, since the 1970s, regardless of whether faculty were teaching first-year composition or technical writing genres in mechanical engineering, the common central concept and practice was writing process. In general, the teaching of writing process took two forms: the first, called writing to learn and including genres like journals and notebooks, whose intent was to use writing as a means of learning; and a second, typically attuned to using writing as a means of assessing learning in higher stakes tasks like case studies, research reports, or capstone projects, each of which required multiple drafts, peer review, and directed feedback, whose general intent was to inculcate writing as a process in college students and to enhance their writing performance. In brief, students were—and continue to be—asked to engage in writing processes both to learn and to demonstrate learning. In fact, one of the distinguishing features between writing in high school contexts and college writing contexts is the elaborated writing process that students develop in their first-year composition courses (Fulkerson, 2005; Yancey et al., 2014) and that they then repurpose for writing tasks in their other classes (Hilgers, Hussey, & Stitt-Bergh, 1999; Jarratt, Mack, & Watson, 2005). The research has shown that students do transfer writing processes from first-year composition into the other classes (Yancey et al., 2014); sometimes, students abbreviate those processes, and often they adapt them. It's worth emphasizing this finding because it means that (a) the claim that Perkins and Salomon (1992) made more than 20 years ago, that we can teach for transfer, is supported by the data showing that writing process has been taught across the college years and the curriculum, and students do transfer process; and (b) when faculty (of all ranks) consistently teach a central concept or process, even within large institutions and across a wide diversity of institutions, students will take it and adapt it, in this case taking what they learned in first-year composition about writing process and repurposing it for other sites of writing—sometimes in general education classes, other times in the major, and still other times in internships.[2]

Currently, there are other concepts and writing practices, in addition to writing process, that researchers in writing studies have identified as important for transfer of knowledge and practice, among them, as the *Elon Statement* asserts, "focusing on rhetorically-based concepts, asking students to engage in metacognitive awareness, and explicitly modeling transfer-focused thinking." Rhetorically based concepts like genre, for example, have shown promise in helping students see both similarities and differences across sites of writing (Yancey et al., 2014), and the ability to articulate such differences and similarities has been identified as a trait of a successful college writer (Navarre Cleary, 2013; Yancey et al., 2014).[3] Likewise, metacognition, and specifically reflection, is cited by generalist transfer researchers (e.g., Bransford, Pellegrino, & Donovan, 2000), as well as by researchers in writing studies (Beaufort, 2007; Sommers, 2011; Yancey, 1998), as a practice assisting students to articulate what they have learned and thus to make the learning their own. In the National Research Council–produced volume *How People Learn* (Bransford et al., 2000), for example, metacognition is identified as essential to learning, in part because even experts use it in defining and addressing problems:

The ability to monitor one's approach to problem solving—to be metacognitive—is an important aspect of the expert's competence. Experts step back from their first, oversimplistic interpretation of a problem or situation and question their own knowledge that is relevant. People's mental models of what it means to be an expert can affect the degree to which they learn throughout their lifetimes. A model that assumes that experts know all the answers is very different from a model of the accomplished novice, who is proud of his or her achievements and yet also realizes that there is much more to learn. (p. 50)

In this construct of learning, a critical maneuver includes monitoring one's learning and questioning one's own knowledge. Likewise, writing studies scholar Anne Beaufort (2007) identified metacognition, or reflection, as the thinking process students can use to review writing problems in terms of their similarities and differences to other writing problems they have tackled:

Literally thinking about thinking, meta-cognition implies vigilant attention to a series of high-level questions as one is in the process of writing: how is this writing task similar to others? Or different? What is the relationship of this writing problem to the larger goals and values of the discourse community in which the text will be received? These and other reflection-in-action kinds of questions, if part of a writer's process, will increase the ability of the writer to learn new writing skills, applying existing skills and knowledge appropriately (i.e., accomplishing positive transfer or learning). (p. 152)

Beaufort thus identified reflection as a component of the curriculum directly related to transfer, to the "applying [of] new writing skills, [of] applying existing skills and knowledge appropriately (i.e., accomplishing positive transfer or learning)"[4] (p. 152).

ePortfolios Designed for Transfer: The Transfer-Bridging Portfolio

Reflection—a process by which we make our own knowledge—is also at the center of portfolio practice, regardless of medium. The defining practices of print portfolios—collection, selection, and reflection (Yancey, 1992)—have migrated onto the web to provide similar a definition of key practices for ePortfolios. In this definition, *portfolios* are a collection of work, a selection or subset of a larger archive, and a group of works—in the case of *eportfolios* for writing across the college years, texts ranging across a wide range of genres and file types—contextualized by the student in a reflection-in-presentation: "the process of articulating the relationships between and among the multiple variables of writing and the writer in a specific context for a specific audience" (Yancey, 1998, p. 200). In addition, even in the era of print portfolios, the potential of portfolios to provide a site of learning crossing multiple contexts—for our purposes, in general education classes, courses in the major, and co- and extracurriculars—was apparent, if not always tapped. As Yancey and Weiser (1997) explained in the introduction to *Situating Portfolios: Four Perspectives*, portfolios have the potential to bridge multiple contexts: "We see bridging portfolios inviting students—from high school to law school—to make a whole text from the fragments of their academic and non-academic experiences, to include in their school work new, real exigence [or purpose] and new, real audiences" (p. 5). Given our more recent interest in transfer, such portfolios, what Yancey and Weiser termed *bridging portfolios*, can be expanded to invite students not only "to make a whole text" from their multiple writing experiences but also to use the portfolio as an explicit site for *transfer thinking*: for locating and reflecting on similarities and differences across writing tasks and thus to facilitate their own transfer of knowledge and practice.

How we might scaffold such a portfolio—what we might call a *transfer-bridging portfolio*—is a good question, but a basic structure could be fairly straightforward. For example, a student would

- create a portfolio early in the first term in college, drawing on a set of tasks and questions related to (a) prior writing experiences (e.g., writing in high school, in community college, in the workplace, in personal life); (b) the new college environment, its unique mission, and the writing tasks students have encountered there; and (c) a dialogue between the two;
- continue, in that first year, to focus on new writing practice and knowledge, in a first-year composition class, in classes in general education, and in other sites of writing (e.g., first-year experiences, co- and extracurriculars, the workplace, study abroad, civic writing), with reflective questions keyed to the following factors directly connected to transfer of writing knowledge and practice: (a) writing processes; (b) writing genres; (c) similarities across tasks; (d) differences across tasks; and (e) kinds of repurposings the student has attempted, how successful they have been, and what the student has learned in the process;
- continue to document and reflect on writing tasks, practices, and concepts during the sophomore year;
- create, in the case of community college students, a culminating reflection to accompany the portfolio that looks both backward at the college writing experience writ large and forward to the student's anticipated writing experiences;

- begin to document and reflect, in the case of the four-year college student, on the transition into the major and the kinds of writing characterizing the major;
- continue to document and reflect on the role of writing in the major and on the factors initiated previously; and
- create, at the conclusion of the degree, a capstone portfolio that provides an opportunity to look back and to look forward into the transition into post-baccalaureate life.

Obviously, such a scaffold raises many questions. Is this the best structure? How does the rhythm outlined here support students? How might such a rhythm vary? How many artifacts are students collecting? What is the range of genres they are responsible for collecting, and how can we be sure that the curriculum introduces them to this range? Do students get credit for this ePortfolio work? Who responds to this work, when, and for what purpose? Given that reflection is a social activity—indeed, there are efforts now to create a social life of reflection inside the curriculum (Yancey, 2014)—how do we provide the interaction that ensures that it is so? More generally, the scaffold offered here may simply function as a prompt to create a better design: that's to the good. At the same time, a point has been made: If we want students to transfer, they need a curricular site where they can engage in such synthesis, such transfer thinking, and the reflection contextualizing it. Typically, colleges and universities do not offer such a site, which for purposes of transfer involving multiple contexts would need to (a) accommodate multiple kinds of writing, (b) occur at the intersection of multiple sites of writing, and (c) continue throughout the life of a student's career; the ePortfolio is ideally equipped to serve this purpose.

The Role of Policy and Funding

Given the needs described previously and the role that ePortfolios can play in hosting and fostering transfer thinking, the way forward is fairly clear. It is reasonable—given the national interest in retention and graduation, in writing as a mechanism for progression through college, in transfer as the process proficient writers engage in, and in the ePortfolio as a site to foster all these goals—to expect educational policy to support the bridging transfer ePortfolio; it's also reasonable to expect that funding would accompany such policy. This policy and funding could operate on two levels at least, and in fact, the two levels might work together.[5] The first, most immediate level is the institutional level: Individual colleges and universities can provide funding for pilot programs, especially those informed by student perspectives,

alumni perspectives, and institutional data keyed to retention and graduation. Other like projects—the ePortfolio at LaGuardia Community College—have reported positive results in all three areas.

The second level, the U.S. policy context is, of course, a tougher nut
to crack. Compared to systems of higher education around the world, the
U.S.'s lack of provision of financial support for educational policy is a bit
odd. Other governments, worldwide, support promising and innovative educational practices with policy and resources. And indeed, there was a time
when the United States did provide such support, even if the funding was
limited: One of the most promising print portfolio programs, for example,
was hosted at Miami University of Ohio, focused on writing, and was funded
by the Fund for the Improvement of Postsecondary Education (FIPSE) in
the early 1990s. Of course, if we believe that the federal government should
not set national higher education policy, that's another matter—as long as
we understand that setting no policy is itself, of course, a policy. And of
course, if we believe that the federal government should not provide funding
for promising educational innovations keyed to national higher educational
priorities, that's another matter as well, one that makes it more difficult to
compete in what is already a globalized economy. But if we believe that educational policy and financial support should contribute to college students'
increased retention and graduation, then what is outlined here is an effort to
be supported, and for the following primary reasons: (a) the role of writing in
securing knowledge, (b) the data showing that writing does transfer, (c) the
need for a site where transfer and transfer thinking can be the prime goal, and
(d) portfolios as that site.

Notes

1. For a good example of a program where students explicitly connect general
education and the major, see the University of Massachusetts's integrative experience
requirement.

2. For a detailed summary of this research, please see Yancey, Robertson, and
Taczak's (2014) *Writing Across Contexts: Transfer, Composition, and Sites of Writing*,
especially chapter 1. Likewise, it's worth considering how tall a benchmark such
as transfer is, given the diversity of writing tasks and genres students are assigned
in their college careers; see, for example, the writing enriched curriculum (WEC)
program at the University of Minnesota for a collection of departmental writing
programs keyed to disciplinary genres and outcomes.

3. As important, students can see differences between their out-of-school writing tasks—in the workplace, for instance—and their school tasks, so the experiences
they may be drawing from are diverse. See, for example, Navarre Cleary (2013) and
Roozen (2010).

4. For evidence of the ways that reflection is used by students to make knowledge in the context of prior knowledge, see Leaker and Ostman (2010, 2016). At the same time, we are still researching the efficacy of different curricular approaches to reflection for the purposes of assisting with transfer of writing knowledge and practice—identifying, for example, which questions students should consider, and how questions should be sequenced, at what points in a given term we might stage them, and what feedback should be provided. For some promising approaches, see Yancey's (1998) *Reflection in the Writing Classroom*; Sommers's (2011) "Reflection Revisited: The Class Collage"; Yancey, Robertson, and Taczak's (2014) *Writing Across Contexts*; and Yancey's (2016) *A Rhetoric of Reflection*.

5. Other forms of collective support are possible, as well, of course, from professional organizations, for example, and regional consortia.

References

Beaufort, A. (2007). *College writing and beyond: A new framework for university writing instruction*. Logan, UT: Utah State University Press.

Bransford, J. D., Pellegrino, J. W., & Donovan, M. S. (Eds.) (2000). *How people learn: Brain, mind, experience, and school* (Expanded ed.). Washington, DC: National Academies Press.

Elon Statement on Writing Transfer. (2015). Retrieved from www.centerforengaged learning.org/elon-statement-on-writing-transfer/

Eynon, B. (2009). Making connections: The LaGuardia ePortfolio. In D. Cambridge, B. Cambridge, & K. B. Yancey (Eds.), *Electronic portfolios 2.0: Emergent research on implementation and impact* (pp. 59–69). Washington, DC: Stylus.

Fulkerson, R. (2005). Composition at the turn of the twenty-first century. *College Composition and Communication, 56*(4), 654–687.

Hilgers, T., Hussey, E., & Stitt-Bergh, M. (1999). As you're writing, you have these epiphanies. *Written Communication, 16*, 317–353.

Jarratt, S., Mack, K., & Watson, S. (2005). *Retrospective writing histories*. Paper presented at the Writing Research Across Borders conference, Santa Barbara, CA.

Leaker, C., & Ostman, H. (2010). Composing knowledge: Writing, rhetoric, and reflection in prior learning assessment. *College Composition and Communication, 61*, 691–717.

Leaker, C., & Ostman, H. (2016). Reflecting practices: Competing models of reflection in the rhetoric of prior learning assessment. In K. B. Yancey (Ed.), *A rhetoric of reflection*. Logan, UT: Utah State University Press.

Navarre Cleary, M. (2013). Flowing and freestyling: Learning from adult students about process knowledge transfer. *College Composition and Communication, 64*, 661–687.

Perkins, D. N., & Salomon, G. (1992). Transfer of learning. In T. N. Postlethwaite & T. Husen (Eds.), *International encyclopedia of education* (2nd ed.). Oxford,

UK: Pergamon. Retrieved from http://learnweb.harvard.edu/alps/thinking/docs/traencyn.htm

Roozen, K. (2010). Tracing trajectories of practice: Repurposing in one student's developing disciplinary writing processes. *Written Communication, 27*, 318–354.

Sommers, J. (2011). Reflection revisited: The class collage. *Journal of Basic Writing, 30*, 99–129.

Yancey, K. B. (Ed.). (1992). *Portfolios in the writing classroom.* Urbana, IL: National Council of Teachers of English.

Yancey, K. B. (1998). *Reflection in the writing classroom.* Logan, UT: Utah State University Press.

Yancey, K. B. (2009). Reflection and electronic portfolios: Inventing the self and reinventing the university. In D. Cambridge, B. Cambridge, & K. B. Yancey (Eds.), *Electronic portfolios 2.0: Emergent research on implementation and impact* (pp. 5–17). Washington, DC: Stylus.

Yancey, K. B. (2014). The social life of reflection: Notes toward an ePortfolio-based model of reflection. In M. Ryan (Ed.), *Teaching reflective learning in higher education* (pp. 189–202). New York, NY: Springer.

Yancey, K. B. (Ed.). (2016). *A rhetoric of reflection.* Logan, UT: Utah State University Press.

Yancey, K. B., Robertson, L., & Taczak, K. (2014). *Writing across contexts: Transfer, composition, and sites of writing.* Logan, UT: Utah State University Press.

Yancey, K. B., & Weiser, I. (1997). Introduction. In K. B. Yancey & I. Weiser (Eds.), *Situating portfolios: Four perspectives* (pp. 1–17). Logan, UT: Utah State University Press.

5

WRITING HIGH-IMPACT PRACTICES

Developing Proactive Knowledge in Complex Contexts

Peter Felten

I n 2008, George Kuh synthesized a wide range of higher education research to identify 10 high-impact practices (HIPs) that "have been widely tested and have been shown to be beneficial for college students from many backgrounds" (p. 9). Kuh's analysis focused on practices that, across a wide range of campuses and contexts, yield increased rates of both student engagement and retention (see Table 5.1).

In explaining this list, Kuh initially noted six factors that make these practices particularly effective. All of these practices demand students invest time and effort in educationally purposeful activities, and all require students to work closely and meaningfully with faculty and peers. For the purposes of this chapter, Kuh's fifth factor is most significant:

> Participation in these activities provides opportunities for students to see how what they are learning works in different settings, on and off campus. These opportunities to integrate, synthesize, and apply knowledge are essential to deep, meaningful learning experiences. (Kuh, 2008, p. 17)

Kuh and O'Donnell (2013) later divided this item into two parts when outlining the essential elements of any HIP: "Periodic, structured opportunities to reflect and integrate learning" and "opportunities to discover relevance of learning through real-world applications" (p. 10). Although neither Kuh (2008) nor Kuh and O'Donnell (2013) used the term *transfer* in their analyses, their language suggests that transfer is a central factor in making any educational practice high impact.

TABLE 5.1
High-Impact Practices

First-year seminars and experiences	Learning communities
Common intellectual experiences	Writing-intensive courses
Collaborative assignments and projects	Undergraduate research
Service-learning/community-based learning	Diversity/global learning
Capstone courses and projects	Internships

Note. See G. Kuh, 2008, *High-Impact Educational Practices: What They Are, Who Has Access to Them, and Why They Matter,* Washington, DC: Association of American Colleges & Universities.

Explicit attention to transfer in the implementation of HIPs has the potential to substantially enhance student learning. As the research outlined in this volume suggests, writing is an essential pedagogy for supporting transfer in (and beyond) HIPs because it prompts students to critically analyze their prior knowledge in new contexts. Careful attention to teaching for writing transfer also can make many educational activities, in and out of the classroom, into high-impact experiences for students.

Transfer and Proactive Knowledge

Transfer, defined most simply, is "the ability to extend what has been learned in one context to new contexts" (Bransford, Brown, & Cocking, 2000, p. 51). In educational settings, including many college and university classrooms, students most often are required to perform what experts call *near transfer* by applying what they learned in a lecture, from a reading, or in a laboratory to answer a question or solve a problem presented on an exam. Sometimes students must become proficient in *far transfer* to adapt what they have learned to address a distinctly different task or question within a discipline (Perkins & Salomon, 1988). This routine academic work often demonstrates if students possess certain knowledge or have mastered specific skills, but such work rarely indicates that students thoughtfully make (or are challenged to make) learning connections across different contexts. Perkins and Salomon (1988) referred to this mindful abstraction and application in new settings as *high-road transfer,* as opposed to *low-road transfer* that is possible with more or less rote application of learning in a familiar context.

Drawing on these insights, Perkins (1998) outlined three conceptions of knowledge that have distinct implications for scholars and practitioners interested in transfer and HIPs. A *possessive conception* views knowledge as discrete units of learning that a student accumulates, like money in a bank. By contrast, a *performative conception* assumes that understanding is a process of applying and using what you know. Performance requires possession, of course, but it goes further to consider how you use what you know. This performative framework is the foundation for much teaching and assessment in higher education. Students who do well at university often become highly proficient at this kind of learning. A fundamental limit of this conception, however, is that performative knowledge typically is explicitly cued; even in rigorous higher education settings, a student demonstrates her understanding of physics, history, or nursing within the context of an exam on or assignment in physics, history, or nursing, respectively. The setting of the performance makes it apparent to students what knowledge they will need to access and apply.

Although possessive and performative knowledge have utility, Perkins considered *proactive knowledge* to be the ultimate goal of education. Proactive knowledge stretches beyond what might be seen as far transfer within a discipline: "The central business of proactive knowledge is not so much analogical application to remote domains as it is direct application to weakly cued circumstances" (Perkins, 2008, p. 8). Inside the classroom, learning is typically demonstrated by specific performance on demand: write an essay answering this question, solve that problem, reflect on the meaning of a certain dilemma. Outside a classroom, however, contexts often provide only limited hints about what sort of knowledge might be necessary to solve a novel problem. As a student listens to a political candidate's speech, should she be drawing on her knowledge of history, rhetoric, political science, and psychology or perhaps some combination of all of those at once? Proactive knowledge is built on alert attention and active curiosity because it occurs without supporting structures that guide performance. Walker (2013, p. 248) explained, "This is effortful and requires conscious thought; there are gaps in both possessive and performative knowledge that have to be filled in a process of active engagement with ideas and concepts." As Perkins (2008, p. 5) concluded, "Knowledge needs to function proactively if it is to function at all."

Writing is a particularly powerful tool for encouraging and supporting this "effortful . . . engagement with ideas and concepts." Well-structured writing assignments foster the application of disciplinary knowledge in complex contexts and the development of metacognitive awareness, challenging students to use their knowledge proactively. When faculty collaboratively "teach for transfer" by scaffolding writing assignments throughout an academic program or a series of HIPs (Principle 4), students will be even more likely to develop proactive knowledge.

Proactive Knowledge, Writing, and High-Impact Practices

Many HIPs immerse students in settings that require proactive knowledge because they do *not* explicitly cue students to apply specific content or skills to address a well-defined problem. Instead they present open-ended situations that students must navigate with far less guidance than they receive in a typical classroom. This section will briefly explore how student learning from four HIPs—undergraduate research, learning communities, service-learning/community-based learning, and internships—requires the development and use of proactive knowledge, as well as how teaching for writing transfer can support that development.

Undergraduate research (UR) practices differ across the disciplines, but students usually pursue independent scholarly inquiry or creative activity with guidance from a faculty mentor (Kinkead, 2005; Kuh & O'Donnell, 2013). Because UR involves students in all aspects of the research process, from problem definition to dissemination, and because UR is rooted in authentic investigation, students learn in fundamentally different ways in UR than they do in most classes. One chemistry student, for instance, described expecting UR "to be like my organic chemistry lab that I just finished last year. . . . I'm used to 'here is the procedure, now get to it,'" but finding the actual research process to not be like that at all because it is simultaneously more open, frustrating, and exciting (quoted in Linn, Palmer, Baranger, Gerard, & Stone, 2015, p. 12617571). UR students move beyond their possessive and performative knowledge of a discipline to wrestle with proactive conceptions of knowledge in the field, requiring them not only to transfer what they learned in the classroom to new settings but also to adapt and use that knowledge in relatively unstructured and uncued ways. Writing for an authentic, often scholarly, audience is an integral part of most undergraduate research experiences, creating the opportunity for students both to apply their new knowledge in a disciplinary genre and to reflect metacognitively on what and how they learned from UR.

Learning communities (LC) have been widely embraced in higher education, although how this HIP is implemented varies considerably. In general, this practice involves "an intentionally developed community that exists to promote and maximize the individual and shared learning of its members. There is ongoing interaction, interplay, and collaboration among the community's members as they strive for specified common learning goals" (Lenning, Hill, Saunders, Solan, & Stokes, 2013, p. 7). Although LCs have shared aims, students learn within complex and dynamic social contexts that are mediated by a variety of forces, including the physical setting, organizational factors, social climate, and personal characteristics of the students, faculty, and staff who make up the community (Jessup-Anger, 2015). Effective LCs transform possessive and performative knowledge by creating opportunities for students to link discrete courses and apply what they are learning in new ways to questions and problems that matter within a particular community (Brownell & Swaner, 2010). The strongest LCs often use writing to support students in individual and collaborative meaning-making linked to the academic and personal goals of the community (Brower & Inklas, 2010), requiring students also to adapt their writing practices to meet the community's shared expectations.

Service-learning/community-based learning (SL/CBL) also is employed in many higher education institutions, although particular practices differ. Most often, SL/CBL aims to advance learning goals and community purposes by bringing together students, faculty and staff, and community partners to work toward shared objectives (Felten & Clayton, 2011). SL/CBL prompts students to come face-to-face with complex individuals, communities, and social realities that offer ill-defined challenges and unfamiliar or dynamic social contexts. The combination of academic, personal, and civic outcomes demonstrated to result from SL/CBL underscores how this HIP encourages students to develop proactive knowledge that connects across domains and that can be applied in unfamiliar settings (Brownell & Swaner, 2010; Warren, 2012). Research on SL/CBL demonstrates not only that writing is an effective tool to promote student outcomes in this HIP but also that students actually learn to be more effective writers in SL/CBL contexts (Wurr, 2002), in part because they have opportunities to practice adapting their writing knowledge for new contexts with authentic audiences and purposes.

Internship, sometimes called work-based or work-integrated learning, "is a form of experiential learning that integrates knowledge and theory learned in the classroom with practical application and skills development in a professional setting" (National Association of Colleges and Employers, 2011). The academic purpose of internship, most basically, is to provide rich, engaging, authentic, and contextualized learning opportunities for students (Freudenberg, Brimble, & Cameron, 2010). Transfer is thus a fundamental goal of most internship programs as students are immersed in environments that prompt them to see how (and whether) what they have learned in school applies in different settings and with diverse groups of people—and, in turn, how learning in an internship connects to academic disciplines (Eyler, 2009; Narayanan, Olk, & Fukami, 2010). The authentic context of an internship requires students to move beyond possessive or performative knowledge to think and write in ways that are much more loosely cued than they are in their classrooms (Anson & Forsberg, 1990).

Other HIPs, such as diversity/global learning, clearly fit into this same pattern of putting students in low-cue contexts that require proactive knowledge. A few HIPs, such as first-year seminars or capstone courses, might seem to be exceptions to this rule because they exist within the typically high-cue context of college classrooms. However, even in these more traditional academic contexts, students can learn to take a proactive approach to knowledge if writing assignments encourage them to become "agents of integration" (Nowacek, 2011) by prompting them to be self-conscious about themselves as writers, to write in a variety of different contexts for varied audiences and purposes, and to reflect on the writing knowledge the context calls on them to adapt and repurpose (Yancey, Robertson, & Taczak, 2014).

Designing for Proactive Knowledge

HIPs consistently are powerful for students of all backgrounds at all sorts of institutions because they prioritize proactive knowledge. HIPs immerse students in authentic learning environments with relatively few clues and structures to guide them in deciding what and how they should transfer what they learned in the classroom into the new context. The dynamic uncertainty of most HIPs leads students to be thoughtful and creative about how they adapt and apply their existing knowledge. This combination of low cue and high metacognition aligns with proactive conceptions of knowledge and fosters high-road transfer.

To maximize the positive outcomes of HIPs, faculty and staff must design these experiences to focus on proactive knowledge. In a foundational report analyzing HIP outcomes, Kuh lamented,

> Within a given type of HIP, such as learning communities or service-learning courses, not all are equal in terms of their quality and impact on students due to variations in overall design, expectations for student performance, nature of assignments and in-class and out-of-class activities, and frequency of feedback, among other factors. (Kuh & O'Donnell, 2013, p. 7)

To ensure quality HIPs, the faculty and staff who create and teach with these practices must support students in navigating these challenging contexts. Doing this requires attention to three important moments for students in any HIP.

First, students need to be prepared for an experience that, unlike much of their prior schoolwork, will have fewer explicit cues about what and how they are to learn. This preparation involves developing the possessive and performative knowledge necessary to operate in the new context, of course, but it also requires students to expect to be uncertain and confused and to be willing and able to persist despite their discomfort. Learning often is troublesome to students, evoking emotional reactions that could spark either intense engagement or real fear (Felten, 2016). Faculty and staff should help students set realistic expectations about what they will encounter during an HIP and should help them prepare to respond in ways that will facilitate learning despite any bumps along the road.

Second, students need to have reflective capacities and guidance throughout their HIP experience. To learn from their HIP experiences, students must be or become mindful about what and how they are encountering in the context of an HIP. Opportunities for structured reflection are essential throughout an HIP to support student meaning-making. Research on student writers, for example, has made clear that prompting students to develop reflective habits about their own writing helps them cultivate the proactive knowledge necessary to write effectively in different genres and for different audiences (Yancey et al., 2014). As Merriam (2004) concluded, "Effective learning follows not from a positive experience but from effective reflection" (p. 62). Faculty and staff should guide students through reflective processes as part of any HIP.

Third, after the HIP concludes, students need to be supported in the process of integrating their learning from that context with their other academic experiences, their professional aspirations, and their evolving sense of identity. This is challenging work, but Sullivan's (2014) analysis of an 88-institution study concluded that post-experience reflection on learning has powerful outcomes for undergraduates: "Practiced in multiple settings, orally and in writing, both within and outside the formal curriculum, [structured reflective] activities helped students integrate academic learning and practical experience with important dimensions of meaning in their lives" (p. 11). Sullivan's research emphasized that integrative learning is likely to happen when students are supported in narrating their own stories about struggle and persistence in complex environments, developing proactive knowledge in the process.

Proactive Knowledge Beyond High-Impact Practices

Designing for proactive knowledge not only will enhance student learning from HIPs but also has the potential to transform student learning across the curriculum. Bass (2012) argued that higher education is in the process of "disrupting ourselves" because our structures and practices are not rooted in what we now know about student learning. In this view, echoed by Kuh and O'Donnell (2013), HIPs exist on the margins of too many campuses, while outdated pedagogies—and conceptions of knowledge—dominate the curriculum. The historian Mark Carnes (2014) critiqued the vast majority of teaching in colleges and universities when he concluded, "Well-intentioned teachers, seeking to create positive classroom experiences, often err in creating activities with little or no risk of failure" (p. 175).

To learn meaningfully, students need to be immersed in experiences, in and out of the classroom, that challenge them to learn and adapt to novel and changing conditions. Learning in and from low-cue environments is most likely to occur when students are supported to reflect critically and metacognitively about their experiences (Ash & Clayton, 2009). As research in this volume demonstrates, writing is a powerful tool to do just that, particularly when faculty and staff work together to teach for transfer by scaffolding student learning across multiple courses and experiences. Rather than aiming for possessive or performative knowledge in isolated settings, we should focus on a more difficult but rewarding target, cultivating proactive knowledge in all of our students throughout their entire university experience.

References

Anson, C., & Forsberg, L. (1990). Moving beyond the academic community: Transitional stages in professional writing. *Written Communication, 7*(2), 200–231.

Ash, S., & Clayton, P. (2009). Generating, deepening, and documenting learning: The power of critical reflection in applied learning. *Journal of Applied Learning in Higher Education, 1*, 25–48.

Bass, R. (2012, March–April). Disrupting ourselves: The problem of learning in higher education. *EDUCAUSE Review*, 23–33.

Bransford, J., Brown, A., & Cocking, R. (Eds.). (2000). *How people learn: Brain, mind, experience, and school* (Expanded ed.). Washington, DC: National Academy Press.

Brower, A., & Inklas, K. (2010). Living learning programs: One high-impact educational practice we now know a lot about. *Liberal Education, 96*(2), 1–9.

Brownell, J., & Swaner, L. (Eds.). (2010). *Five high-impact practices: Research on learning outcomes, completion, and quality*. Washington, DC: Association of American Colleges & Universities.

Carnes, M. (2014). *Minds on fire: How role-immersion games transform college*. Cambridge, MA: Harvard University Press.

Eyler, J. (2009). The power of experiential education. *Liberal Education, 95*, 24–31.

Felten, P. (2016). On the threshold with students. In R. Land, J. H. F. Meyer, & M. T. Flanagan (Eds.), *Threshold concepts in practice* (pp. 3–10). Rotterdam, the Netherlands: Sense.

Felten, P., & Clayton, P. (2011). Service-learning. In W. Buskist & J. E. Groccia (Eds.), *Evidence-based teaching: New directions for teaching and learning, No. 128* (pp. 75–84). San Francisco, CA: Jossey-Bass.

Freudenberg, B., Brimble, M., & Cameron, C. (2010). Where there is a WIL there is a way. *Higher Education Research and Development, 29,* 575–588.

Jessup-Anger, J. (2015). Theoretical foundations of learning communities. In M. Benjamin (Ed.), *Learning communities from start to finish: New directions for student services, No. 149* (pp. 17–27). San Francisco, CA: Jossey-Bass.

Kinkead, J. (Ed.). (2005). *Valuing and supporting undergraduate research: New directions for teaching and learning, No. 93.* San Francisco, CA: Jossey-Bass.

Kuh, G. (2008). *High-impact educational practices: What they are, who has access to them, and why they matter.* Washington, DC: Association of American Colleges & Universities.

Kuh, G., & O'Donnell, K. (2013). *Ensuring quality and taking high-impact practices to scale.* Washington, DC: Association of American Colleges & Universities.

Lenning, O., Hill, D., Saunders, K., Solan, A., & Stokes, A. (2013). *Powerful learning communities: A guide to developing student, faculty and professional learning communities to improve student success and organizational effectiveness.* Sterling, VA: Stylus.

Linn, M., Palmer, E., Baranger, A., Gerard, E., & Stone, E. (2015). Undergraduate research experiences: Impacts and opportunities. *Science, 347*(6222), 12617571–12617576.

Merriam, S. (2004). The role of cognitive development in Mezirow's transformational learning theory. *Adult Education Quarterly, 55*(1), 60–68.

Narayanan, V., Olk, P., & Fukami, C. (2010). Determinants of internship effectiveness: An exploratory model. *Academy of Management Learning and Education, 9,* 61–80.

National Association of Colleges and Employers. (2011). *Position statement on U.S. internships: A definition and criteria to assess opportunities and determine the implications for compensation.* Retrieved from www.naceweb.org/connections/advocacy/internship_position_paper/

Nowacek, R. (2011). *Agents of integration: Understanding transfer as a rhetorical act.* Carbondale, IL: Southern Illinois University Press.

Perkins, D. (1998). What is understanding? In M. Wiske (Ed.), *Teaching for understanding: Linking research with practice* (pp. 39–57). San Francisco, CA: Jossey-Bass.

Perkins, D. (2008). Beyond understanding. In R. Land, J. H. F. Meyer, & J. Smith (Eds.), *Threshold concepts within the disciplines* (pp. 3–19). Rotterdam, the Netherlands: Sense.

Perkins, D., & Salomon, G. (1988). Teaching for transfer. *Educational Leadership, 46*(1), 22–32.

Sullivan, W. (2014). Exploring vocation: Reframing undergraduate education as a quest for purpose. *Change, 46*(4), 6–13.

Walker, G. (2013). A cognitive approach to threshold concepts. *Higher Education, 65,* 247–263.

Warren, J. (2012). Does service-learning increase student learning? A meta-analysis. *Michigan Journal of Community Service Learning, 18*(2), 56–61.

Wurr, A. (2002). Text-based measures of service-learning writing quality. *Reflections: A Journal of Writing, Service-Learning, and Community Literacy, 2*(2), 41–56.

Yancey, K., Robertson, L., & Taczak, K. (2014). *Writing across contexts: Transfer, composition, and sites of writing.* Logan, UT: Utah State University Press.

6

DIVERSITY, GLOBAL CITIZENSHIP, AND WRITING TRANSFER

Brooke Barnett, Woody Pelton, Francois Masuka, Kevin Morrison,
and Jessie L. Moore

Diversity and global learning are integral parts of twenty-first-century learning. The Association of American Colleges & Universities (AAC&U, n.d.) identified *intercultural knowledge* and *competence* as essential learning outcomes and included a Global Learning rubric in its Valid Assessment of Learning in Undergraduate Education (VALUE) initiative. The Institute of International Education's Open Doors reports have highlighted steady growth in enrollment by international students at U.S. colleges and universities for decades. For both native and international students, higher education is an opportunity to obtain knowledge about diverse cultures, engage in and value intercultural cooperation, and learn to navigate pluralism.

It's not surprising, then, that many university mission statements now promote the preparation of global citizens. Douglas and Jones-Rikkers (2001) identified a global citizen as a global-minded person who values a broadened perspective on various issues; opposes prejudice; and sees viewpoints that differ from their own gender, ethnic, national, sexual orientation, or religious perspectives as equally valid. Hett (1993) identified components of global mindedness as responsibility, cultural pluralism, efficacy, global centrism, and interconnectedness. AAC&U's Global Learning VALUE rubric focuses on global self-awareness, perspective taking, cultural diversity, personal and social responsibility, understanding global systems, and applying knowledge to contemporary global contexts.

Clearly, higher education stakeholders see the benefits of a diverse learning environment, the global citizen aspiration of pluralism, and the promise of transformative learning. Universities must strive to provide clear and evidence-based opportunities for students to learn about themselves and others and to interact positively and productively with people from backgrounds different from their own. Indeed, several academic studies show that students actually learn better by interacting and exchanging ideas with people different from themselves (Gurin, Dey, Hurtado, & Gurin, 2002). We also know that transformative learning requires perspective taking that comes from a focus on diversity and global engagement. Mezirow (2000) defined *transformative learning* as the process whereby "we transform our taken-for-granted frames of reference to make them more inclusive, discriminating, open, and reflective so that they may generate beliefs and opinions that will prove more true or justified to guide action" (p. 214). Mezirow proceeded to explain that for such transformation to occur, students must alter their frame of reference by critically reflecting on their own assumptions and beliefs and striving to think of new ways to define and understand their environment.

Transformation can occur in discrete experiences, such as an on-campus class, a domestic study program, an academic service-learning project, or an internship, or across a series of courses or experiences (Toncar & Cudmore, 2000). Transformation comes in many forms and can include "a moment of transition from passivity to naiveté to some animation and critical awareness" (Shor & Freire, 1987, p. 34). As U.S. universities strive to foster global citizenship, many have pursued global learning course work, increased international student enrollment, and offered study abroad opportunities as initiatives with the potential to showcase difference and promote transformation. To achieve learning outcomes common to the previously described articulations of global citizenship and to make these global learning initiatives most effective, though, universities need innovative learning structures and pedagogical approaches to help students make meaning from these encounters with and studies of human differences.

Writing is a core component of the potential meaning-making that can happen when students encounter or study aspects of human difference, and the Global Learning VALUE rubric integrates several communicative tasks into its capstone benchmarks (AAC&U, n.d.):

- Cultural diversity necessitates "initiating meaningful interaction with other cultures to address significant global problems."
- Understanding global systems requires students to "advocate for informed, appropriate action to solve complex problems in the human and natural worlds."
- Applying knowledge to contemporary global contexts may require "using interdisciplinary perspectives . . . with others." (p. 2)

Collectively, these benchmarks suggest that integrated, transformative, global learning must include the ability to initiate interactions, advocate, and collaborate. In other words, communication is at the heart of global learning and students' development toward global citizenship.

Yet, as forecast by Principle 2, navigating communication norms across diverse cultures and international sites of learning is a complex process. In this chapter, we examine that complexity and discuss how Principle 1 (i.e., successful writing transfer requires transforming or repurposing prior knowledge for a new context) and Principle 4 (i.e., university programs can teach for transfer) can help international program directors, general education coordinators, and other faculty, staff, and administrators help students navigate global learning's challenges and opportunities as students develop as global citizens.

Complexities Students Encounter in Global Learning Initiatives

Both international students and U.S. students face challenges as they navigate global learning initiatives, encountering unfamiliar expectations about ownership of work, often complicated by concurrent calls for collaboration; differences in the necessity for independent study, with varied norms for opportunities for (and expectations around) interaction with faculty; less (or more) frequent assessments; and different access to and types of resources. U.S. institutions, for example, often place value on guarding one's own work rather than on sharing and helping other students, converting what is a virtue in many cultures to "cheating" in the United States. At the same time, U.S. courses often promote group work that requires partnering with other students; group work is less common in other educational systems, and students from diverse cultures often bring different working style dynamics that can cause tensions if faculty do not offer strategies for collaborating, particularly within that individual course context and the faculty member's expectations for group work.

Similarly, the relationship between student and faculty is commonly more formal and less interactive in other cultures (top-down lecture) than in the United States, making it uncomfortable for some international students to ask questions, participate in class, and seek out help from faculty. This expectation of active participation is further complicated when international students feel uncomfortable with their language proficiency and hesitate to express their ideas.

Regular assessment is not as common outside the United States, so U.S. students studying abroad may struggle with new expectations for self-assessment, leading up to a higher stakes cumulative assessment. Similarly, international students may have difficulty understanding "sandwich" feedback because it sounds more positive than it is in reality. The importance of the syllabus as a contract with the faculty is often new to international students, and the availability of support (e.g., writing centers, tutoring, math labs, access to faculty, personal counseling) is helpful but often unexpected and a cultural change. Many international students aren't accustomed to seeking out help and have to learn how to use the resources available.

In addition, writing conventions are contextually situated. Just as expectations for writing can vary from discipline to discipline, different geographic regions and cultural traditions have different conventions for writing. These differences inform the fields of cross-cultural rhetorics, international communications, and second-language writing, but they are rarely acknowledged in students' day-to-day classroom experiences.

It is important to acknowledge that many U.S. colleges and universities—each with some degree of success—have over the years assisted their international students by devoting human and material resources during students' critical transition periods. International students benefit from the support of international student and scholar offices, which provide various services such as advising on cultural adjustment, immigration, and personal and financial issues and offering orientation programs that inform new international students and their dependents about life in the United States.

Despite all the efforts and support from the various offices on U.S. campuses, there is no doubt that, as Glass, Buus, and Braskamp (2013) contended, the quality of the student experience at U.S. universities is uneven, markedly, among students from different countries. But making sure that international students—regardless of their primary languages—learn and master the fundamental skills of writing for academic purposes and develop strategies for transferring writing skills is crucial so that international students are able to fully participate and share their viewpoints in courses and cocurricular activities.

Perhaps more significant, many U.S.-educated students have limited experience speaking in, studying in, or working in contexts that use languages other than English. In a study of undergraduate and graduate students enrolled in language courses or completing degree requirements in their nonnative languages, U.S. undergraduates described writing in Spanish as a second language as like "wearing shoes on the wrong feet, getting [a] wisdom tooth removed, trying to solve the puzzle with missing parts, . . . [and] dancing on razor blades" (Cozart, Wirenfeldt Jensen, Wichmann-Hansen, Kupatadze, & Chiu, 2016, p. 318).

To engage in perspective taking, fully grapple with cultural diversity, and adopt a global centric mind-set, though, students must "dance on razor blades." They must transform or repurpose "prior knowledge (even if only slightly) for a new context in order to adequately meet the expectations of new audiences and fulfill new purposes," not only for writing, the focus of Principle 1 (Moore, this volume), but also for interacting, advocating, and collaborating as global citizens. Fortunately, when universities are attentive to writing transfer, they can help students navigate the cognitive complexity of making meaning across cultures.

Teaching for Transfer to Teach for Global Learning

In addition to being a benchmark of global learning, writing can expand students' experiences with difference, facilitating analysis, reflection, and subsequent discussion. Principle 4 noted,

> University programs . . . can "teach for transfer." Enabling practices that promote writing transfer include constructing writing curricula and classes that focus on the study and practice of rhetorically based concepts (such as genre, purpose, and audience) that prepare students to analyze expectations for writing and learning within specific contexts, asking students to engage in activities that foster the development of metacognitive awareness, and explicitly modeling transfer-focused thinking. (Moore, p. 7, this volume)

Teaching students to analyze rhetorical situations is an integral component of many writing courses. To communicate effectively, writers must have a sense of their audiences' values and concerns, understand the sociocultural context in which they are acting, and consider what types of texts will help them best engage their audiences in the given contexts. Rhetorical analysis strategies, therefore, also function as strategies for understanding global systems; they can scaffold students through "examin[ing] the historical and contemporary roles" to "analyz[ing] major elements of global systems" to "us[ing] deep knowledge of the historic and contemporary role and differential effects of human organizations and actions on global systems," progressive markers of "Understanding Global Systems" in the Global Learning VALUE rubric.

Next, we offer examples of teaching for transfer to teach for global learning in three key areas: course content, international student enrollment, and study away.

Course Content

Many college courses focus on cultural difference in a comparative U.S.-based and international- or domestic-based context, a key to learning in the twenty-first century (Bennett & Bennett, 2004, p. 148). Intergroup Relations

Dialogue and Reacting to the Past are well-researched pedagogies with impressive outcomes (Davison & Goldhaber, 2007; Dessel & Rogge, 2008; Kelly, 2009; Maxwell, Nagda, & Thompson, 2011). For many universities, the stated promise of global citizenship means an ultimate goal for every student to study aspects of culture individually and often through courses in a liberal-arts-based general education curriculum. For some universities, this goal is pursued through a specifically designated diversity course, and at others, distribution categories in general education focus heavily on culture and human difference.

In addition to systematically integrating authentic writing into courses that examine cultural difference, institutions of higher education must be attentive to how they teach writing. For both U.S.-educated students and international students, integrating explicit teaching for transfer of writing knowledge better prepares students for future writing success and for global citizenship. Learning to ask questions about new writing contexts also prepares students to inquire about the social–cultural diversity among those contexts. Asking, "Who is my audience, and what do I know about their values and beliefs?" reinforces students' perspective taking, value of cultural diversity, and analysis of global systems. Asking, "What is my purpose, and what writing tools will best enable me to achieve that purpose given my audience?" prompts students to make informed choices as they "address ethical, social, and environmental challenges in global systems," a capstone benchmark in AAC&U's Global Learning VALUE rubric. Several of this volume's Critical Sites of Impact cases offer examples of teaching for transfer curricula that would support these outcomes.

International Student Enrollment

While adjusting to cultural, social, and learning environments in a new country, many international students in higher education encounter various barriers that may impede their full participation in classes and campus life. When international students are nonnative speakers, they are trying to understand a lecture, a group project, an assignment, or an assigned reading in a second or third language. Understanding lectures and course discussions would be difficult enough if all faculty and classmates spoke in a uniform and easily understood form of English. U.S. speakers use several varieties and regional dialects of English, though, resulting in variations in accent and speed. Even for international students who are native speakers of English, the classroom use of American idioms (e.g., a stitch in time, Uncle Sam, carpetbagger) and the expectation that students are familiar with American sports, geography, personalities, and folklore often require students to engage in far transfer of cultural knowledge that they might not have.

Understandably, most U.S. colleges and universities begin the teaching of writing based on two assumptions: that they are teaching native speakers of English and that those students come from a U.S. high school (or home schooled) education. Many international students are missing one or both of those foundations, so offering multiple placement options for first-year writing courses, one of the most commonly required general education courses across U.S. universities, enables students to select types of instructional support that best meet their needs. Placement options can include "mainstream" first-year writing courses designed primarily for native English speakers (NES), ESL writing courses, and cross-cultural composition courses "designed to include more or less equal numbers of ESL and NES students . . . to foster cross-cultural understanding, communication, and collaboration" (Silva, 1994, p. 40). Cross-cultural composition classes are designed not only to adapt writing instruction to both ESL and NES students' needs to support writing-related learning outcomes but also to promote intercultural understanding (Matsuda & Silva, 1999). When universities are able to offer a range of course options for satisfying writing requirements, placement decisions should be based on direct assessments of students' writing proficiency, not on standardized test scores; directed self-placement allows students to make an informed choice about their course selection (Conference on College Composition and Communication, 2014).

Study Away

Study away experiences like study abroad and domestic off campus study (including service-learning) are experiential learning opportunities that can facilitate students having meaningful interactions with people unlike themselves. Reflection and writing about the experience provides students the opportunity to make meaning and develop intercultural skills. Byram (1997, p. 34) suggested outcomes from such experiences are "knowledge of others; knowledge of self; skills to interpret and relate; skills to discover and/or to interact; valuing others' values, beliefs, and behaviors; and relativizing one's self." Byram's definition of *cultural competency* can form the basis for students' reflection about interest in knowing other people's way of life and introducing one's own culture to others, ability to change perspective, knowledge about one's own and others' culture for intercultural communication, and knowledge about intercultural communication processes. Common elements of intercultural competence include "the awareness, valuing, and understanding of cultural differences; experiencing other cultures; and self-awareness of one's own culture. These common elements stress the underlying importance of cultural awareness, both of one's own as well as others' cultures" (Deardorff, 2006, p. 247) and understanding of the intersectionality of identity (Abes, Jones, & McEwen, 2007; Renn, 2004; Torres, 2009).

The experiential nature of study abroad lends itself to a variety of modes when it comes to written work. Faculty often assign journals, blogs, or short written reflections as a means of assessing student engagement with the local culture. Absent a real audience, students often perceive these assignments as "easier," requiring less depth and therefore less effort on their part. When faculty ask students to engage with a real audience as they write these reflections, though, the clear writing context creates opportunities for them to talk about audience expectations for evidence of the students' thoughts and observations. Writing for a real audience also discourages students' rushing to finish the writing assignment, rather than doing it well, because students begin to care about how their audience will read and understand their work.

Much of what students write when assigned a blog or a journal is descriptive in nature. Students are great at soaking up the study abroad experience and reporting it in written form. Some describe in great detail what they are seeing or doing, often re-creating the experience quite vividly for the reader. Unfortunately, this is often where the writing stops. Students seldom dig deeper on their own, failing to draw comparisons to their own cultural frames of reference. Also, there is rarely much deep reflection expressed on the cultural underpinnings for much of what they are experiencing. From an intercultural learning standpoint, this is unfortunate. Rhetorical analysis strategies address this gap by helping students use their writing as a way to process their experiences, drawing cultural inferences and extrapolating cultural hypotheses based on their observations as they examine both the context and the people engaged in communication within that context.

By teaching for (writing) transfer to teach for global learning in these contexts and others, universities engage students in careful analysis of global situations and provide opportunities for students to make meaning from their encounters with and studies of human differences. In turn, universities better prepare students to interact, advocate, and collaborate as global citizens.

References

Abes, E. S., Jones, S. R., & McEwen, M. K. (2007). Reconceptualizing the model of multiple dimensions of identity: The role of meaning-making capacity in the construction of multiple identities. *Journal of College Student Development, 48,* 1–22.

American Association of Colleges and Universities. (n.d.). Global Learning VALUE rubric (preview). Retrieved from www.aacu.org/sites/default/files/files/VALUE/GlobalLearning.pdf

Bennett, J. M., & Bennett, M. J. (2004). Developing intercultural sensitivity: An integrative approach to global and domestic diversity. In D. Landis, J. M. Bennett, & M. J. Bennett (Eds.), *Handbook of intercultural training* (pp. 147–164). Thousand Oaks, CA: Sage.

Byram, M. (1997). *Teaching and assessing intercultural communicative competence.* Clevedon, UK: Multilingual Matters.

Conference on College Composition and Communication. (2014). CCCC statement on second language writing and writers. Retrieved from www.ncte.org/cccc/resources/positions/secondlangwriting

Cozart, S. M., Wirenfeldt Jensen, T., Wichmann-Hansen, G., Kupatadze, K., & Chiu, S. (2016). Negotiating multiple identities in second or foreign language writing in higher education. In C. M. Anson & J. L. Moore (Eds.), *Critical transitions: Writing and the question of transfer* (pp. 303–334). Fort Collins, CO: WAC Clearinghouse/University Press of Colorado.

Davison, A., & Goldhaber, S. L. (2007). Integration, socialization, collaboration: Inviting native and non-native English speakers into the academy through "reacting to the past." In J. Summerfield & C. Benedicks (Eds.), *Reclaiming the public university: Conversations on general and liberal education.* New York, NY: Peter Lang.

Deardorff, D. K. (2006). Identification and assessment of intercultural competence as a student outcome of internationalization. *Journal of Studies in International Education, 10,* 241–266.

Dessel, A., & Rogge, M. (2008). Evaluation of intergroup dialogue: A review of the empirical literature. *Conflict Resolution Quarterly, 26*(2), 199–238.

Douglas, C., & Jones-Rikkers, C. G. (2001). Study abroad programs and American student worldmindedness: An empirical analysis. *Journal of Teaching in International Business, 13*(1), 55–66.

Glass, C. R., Buus, S., & Braskamp, L. A. (2013). *Uneven experiences: What's missing and what matters for today's international students.* Chicago, IL: Global Perspective Institute.

Gurin, P., Dey, E. L., Hurtado, S., & Gurin, G. (2002). Diversity and higher education: Theory and impact on educational outcomes. *Harvard Educational Review, 72*(3), 330–366.

Hett, E. J. (1993). Development of an instrument to measure globalmindedness. *Dissertation Abstracts International, 54*(10), 3724.

Kelly, K. A. (2009). A yearlong general education course using "reacting to the past" pedagogy to explore democratic practice. *International Journal of Learning, 16*(11), 147–155.

Matsuda, P. K., & Silva, T. (1999). Cross-cultural composition: Mediated integration of U.S. and international students. *Composition Studies, 27*(1), 15–30.

Maxwell, K. E., Nagda, B., & Thompson, M. (Eds.). (2011). *Facilitating intergroup dialogues: Bridging differences, catalyzing change.* Sterling, VA: Stylus.

Mezirow, J. (2000). *Learning as transformation: Critical perspectives on a theory in progress.* San Francisco, CA: Jossey-Bass.

Renn, K. A. (2004). *Mixed race students in college: The ecology of race, identity, and community.* Albany, NY: State University of New York Press.

Shor, I., & Freire, P. (1987). *A pedagogy of liberation: Dialogues on transforming education*. New York, NY: Bergin and Garvey.

Silva, T. (1994). An examination of writing program administrators' options for the placement of ESL students in the first year writing classes. *WPA: Writing Program Administration, 18*(1–2), 37–43.

Toncar, M. F., & Cudmore, B. V. (2000). The overseas internship experience. *Journal of Marketing Education, 22*(1), 54–63.

Torres, V. (2009). The developmental dimensions of recognizing racism. *Journal of College Student Development, 50*, 504–520.

7

TELLING EXPECTATIONS ABOUT ACADEMIC WRITING

If Not Working, What About Knotworking?

Carmen M. Werder

Ask just about anyone what matters to college success, and he or she will tell you that being able to write well is at or near the top of the list. Even students themselves will often say that writing is crucial not only to succeeding in college but also to *learning well* in college and even to "making the most of college" (Light, 2001, p. 10). In agreement with this clear consensus about the importance of writing, many of us in the academy have also come to know that learning to write proficiently across multiple contexts represents "a complex phenomenon and understanding that complexity is central to facilitating students' successful consequential transitions" (Principle 2). Coming to terms with the complexity of writing, then, represents one of the biggest ongoing challenges, among many, facing us in higher education.

Given the range of stakeholders (students, faculty, administrators, employers, and the public) with a vested interest in college graduates being proficient writers, expectations for what constitutes writing proficiency are bound to vary, and the extent of that variance inevitably contributes to the complexity of understanding writing in any given context. Despite this assumption, we can also safely assume that the more stakeholders share *common expectations* of writing proficiency, the more they can enable it across multiple contexts. And the more stakeholders hold *different expectations* of writing proficiency, the less they can enable it across multiple contexts. But how do we know for sure what these stakeholders' expectations in our own institutions are at any given time?

Background

This chapter traces survey results at my home institution, which revealed a sharp disparity between what writing course faculty and students say they expected in terms of writing proficiency at first-year and upper-division levels and an even more dramatic discrepancy between their views and those of central administrators. Follow-up focus groups and interviews also pointed to conspicuous gaps between what stakeholders said about their expectations for writing proficiency and what they actually meant by the terms. My analysis highlights the importance of recognizing the troubling implications of these contradictions for students trying to traverse the rugged terrain of academic writing and suggests how continually asking stakeholders to talk about their expectations about writing proficiency may be a profound, ongoing way to uncover concerns not only about writing but also about learning generally. Furthermore, I suggest the value of responding to these emergent, inevitable disparities not with traditional modes of institutional collaboration but instead with *knotworking* (Y. Engeström, 2001, 2007, 2008; Engeström, Engeström, & Vähäaho, 1999), a fluid organizational process where no single person, program, or product holds exclusive authority for reconciling contradictions or resolving concerns.[1]

My research project resulted from a simple desire to hear what various stakeholders across my university talked about when they talked about their expectations for academic writers. Like other writing program administrators, I had speculated on what colleagues in multiple contexts at my institution expected writers to know and do, but I didn't have any data to support my speculations. I assumed that there would be gaps in our expectations, misalignments that might point to affordances that could help our student writers move more smoothly from first-year writing to upper-division writing. But my speculations relied solely on a felt sense as I heard (and overheard) conversations over a dozen years as I moved in my role as the director of writing instruction support to offer professional development for faculty teaching in our upper-division writing courses.

Method

Besides demographic information, the survey (with only slight variation in the wording for faculty, students, and administrators) posed essentially one question for open-ended response: *What do you think students need to know and be able to do to be proficient academic writers?* Students in my study came from our required first-year composition course (FYC) and from our upper-division writing proficiency courses (WPC).[2] Faculty included FYC instructors and a sampling of WPC faculty from across disciplines. The central administrators included people like the provost, deans, and directors, as well as chairs of some large departments. To get a macro sense of what these various stakeholders would say about their expectations for academic writers, I surveyed all FYC courses (pre- and post-) for a full academic year (2011–2012), so approximately 2,500 FYC student respondents and 50 FYC instructors. An additional 52 WPC faculty and 126 WPC students from across our 7 colleges responded. The survey to central administrators resulted in 27 respondents. Following the survey, I arranged for 3 mixed-focus groups that were facilitated by a trained program assistant and several interviews with WPC faculty members. Over the course of my study, I also engaged 8 undergraduate students who helped compose the survey and focus group questions and generate coding categories and analyze emerging data.

In analyzing the survey data, I used a grounded theory approach and enlisted the help of two undergraduates per quarter to help develop 16 coding categories. Although the number of categories might seem high, it is worth noting that we started with 30 to 35 categories when the undergraduates working with me simply tried to name the myriad kinds of survey responses they encountered from the first set of surveys. I thought it was telling how the student coinquirers viewed almost every response as a discrete expectation, and as one of them remarked, "No wonder writing is so hard; just look at all the different things you need to know and do." As a writing specialist, I could see through to a common expectation (e.g., the need to "state an opinion" was really the same expectation as to "have a thesis"), whereas the student coders seemed to count everything as a discrete item, suggesting how writing proficiency was such a complex phenomenon for them that every expression of an expectation represented just one discrete component of a huge set of knowledge and skills.

In the end, we whittled the response categories down to 16 (see Table 7.1), though the categories often encompassed an array of also-known-as terms.

Results

Although there was some variation across survey sets, the results revealed that certain groups of stakeholders clearly tended to privilege certain categories over others. The great majority of FYC faculty and students emphasized critical reading and analysis, especially in pre-surveys, and this privileged expectation held steady in post-surveys as well. An intriguing difference is that FYC faculty also tended to emphasize thesis/claim from the get-go (and throughout the term), whereas in pre-surveys FYC students surprisingly emphasized expectations around classroom behavior. This concern with simply being a good, prepared-for-class student—never mind what was expected of them

TABLE 7.1
Coding Categories: Expectations for Proficient Academic Writers

Category Name	Also-Known-As Term
1. Critical analysis	Critical thinking
2. Critical reading	Close reading, coming to terms
3. Composing process	Strategies for prewriting, invention, revising, editing, and so on
4. Evidence	Development, using sources
5. Thesis/claim	Opinion, judgment, overall point
6. Quality of expression	Clarity, concision, accuracy
7. Rhetorical knowledge	Audience, purpose
8. Organization	Structure, transitions, genre, form
9. Application to other contexts	Being able to write for all university courses
10. Vocabulary	Vocabulary about writing, general vocabulary
11. Personal style	Voice, authenticity
12. Conventions	Mechanics, grammar, punctuation, spelling, documentation
13. Attitudes	Perceptions of writing, self-confidence as writer
14. Classroom behavior	Contributing to in-class discussion, being in class every day and on time, following in-class peer response format
15. Generic	Getting better at writing, becoming a stronger writer
16. Metacognition	Self-awareness

as writers—might have resulted from the care with which FYC instructors detailed the expectations in their syllabi for attending class and being prepared given the challenge first-year students have in transitioning from high school to college. This concern with classroom behavior that did not directly reference writing was much more pronounced in pre-survey responses and tended to diminish as the quarter went on and even as the academic year went on. Perhaps this recurring concern with classroom behavior might also reflect students' understanding of how being proficient writers correlates with being disciplined, prepared students. In closing surveys at the end of the term, the emphasis tended to shift away from these general behavior issues to the importance of being able to cite sources, with respondents often referencing the "citation sandwich" (a strategy used in FYC to incorporate source material) as something all academic writers needed to be able to do.

In contrast to FYC faculty, WPC faculty—across many disciplinary contexts—overwhelmingly privileged organization (especially coherence) and evidence (also known as development) above other categories in their survey responses. But the WPC students surveyed talked more about issues of expression such as clarity and concision, as well as the need to know conventions mainly of documentation. What is noteworthy is that in sharp contrast to the FYC faculty and students, absolutely none of the WPC faculty or students spoke to the expectation of critical reading. Although there was some variation in what faculty and students privileged, there was no doubt about what the administrators surveyed expected: 24 of the 27 administrators spoke almost exclusively of surface-level conventions. And there was no doubting what they meant by conventions: sentence-level matters of grammar and punctuation. Many even emphasized the importance of spelling.

Although I have highlighted the privileged categories of expectations, there were also many of the other 16 categories mixed throughout the responses. In fact, all the undergraduates who helped me generate the categories remarked on just *how many* kinds of expectations there were, reflecting how overwhelming academic writing proficiency demands seem for our students. At the same time, there was one category of response that ended up almost empty: metacognition. The conspicuous absence of comments about students' need to be able to articulate how they think about writing was startling. Only a mere 2% of all respondents (and only students) said anything akin to this FYC student's response: "I'll need to be able to explain what's going on in my head when I respond to a writing assignment."

Emerging Concerns

I was prepared to hear FYC students and faculty report expectations on the survey that were different from those of WPC students and faculty, but I wondered in what ways they would be different. I also assumed that central administrators would have yet different expectations, but again I was curious as to how they would be different. I confess that I did entertain a fantasy that there would be many (or at least some) areas of overlap, some common verbiage in how the various stakeholders talked about writing expectations. Ultimately, I was startled by the disparity between what students and faculty privileged at various levels and stunned to see how much their stated expectations differed from those of central administrators—the ones with authority over institutional resources. Furthermore, given what Nowacek (2011) and others have highlighted about the important role of meta-awareness being necessary though not sufficient for transfer, this stark omission was extremely troubling.

Although the misalignment in expectations across groups of stakeholders, as revealed in the survey responses, was disturbing enough, what some of these stakeholders said in focus groups and interviews raised additional concerns, because their articulated expectations were often very different from their tacit ones. As one representative example, here's what one WPC faculty said in an interview about her main expectation for student writers:

> You would think that by the time they are seniors, they would have *basic skills*, like the idea that you need a topic sentence; that the rest of the paragraph relates to the topic sentence; good sentence structure; a sense of audience; how to make an argument. You know, *basic skills*.

The surprisingly expansive interpretation of "basic skills" by this faculty member made me question all the survey responses in terms of what respondents actually meant by the terms they used in articulating their expectations. And to what extent did respondents have any shared meaning around the same terms? What this instructor meant by *basic skills* certainly contrasted with what FYC instructors understood, and this discrepancy highlighted how when it comes to talking about writing proficiency, we likely all use code words and assume that others will decode them as we do.

Ultimately, my data left me puzzled: What did the various stakeholders really mean by *writing proficiency*? When students say they expect to be able to use a "citation sandwich," do they mean that they need to know how to incorporate evidence in advancing a claim or how to put periods in the right place for APA documentation style? Given not only the misalignments between what stakeholders said they expected across various levels but also the gaps between what stakeholders said about their expectations and what they actually meant, it's a wonder students can navigate the white waters of academic writing at all. At the same time, the disparities raised a serious question about *why* we hold writing well in college in such high esteem anyway. In other words, what do various stakeholders think writing proficiency enables learners to do in the world? The FYC survey responses seemed to point to the ultimate value of writing proficiency for being critical thinkers. The WPC responses reflected a belief that writing proficiently would help students express themselves in a well-reasoned, clear, and concise way. The administrators' responses highlighted the value of writing proficiency for enabling students to present themselves appropriately for a public audience. Which stakeholders had the right set of expectations? And if all of them are right and necessary, how might stakeholders collaborate in helping students figure out what they need to know and do to be proficient writers across multiple writing contexts? A knotty problem to be sure.

The Potential of Knotworking

In the process of coming to terms with the results of my study, I came across the notion of *knotworking*, a boundary-crossing approach designed to organize collectively in addressing a learning challenge across activity systems. Grounded in activity theory, knotworking is a conceptual framework to help describe how individual consciousness can be understood by studying practices in an organizational system, and it seeks to temporarily stabilize and address shared concerns (Engeström et al., 1999). By crossing boundaries and gathering around emergent shared concerns, rather than moving from static institutional structures, knotworking represents a way of collaborating in a continuously temporary way to both frame a problem and solve it without relying on a sole, fixed authority. By continuously slipping in and out of knots, individuals "tie with" each other around shared matters of concern rather than use the traditional model of collaboration where a single person in authority tries to "tie down" an answer to a problem—an approach that risks creating a noose for that person. Key to understanding knotworking is viewing it as a form of expansive learning, "that is, the processes by which a work organization resolves its internal contradictions in order to construct qualitatively new ways of working" (Y. Engeström, 2007, p. 23). In this case, knotworking represents a potentially transformative way of addressing the contradictions and misalignments discerned in expectations about writing proficiency across the activity systems of a university.

As a constellation of activity systems, a university is a community of multiple points of view, histories, and interests, so reconciling these competing voices necessarily demands ongoing negotiation (Engeström & Sannino, 2009), as well as a "dialogic approach" that relies on discovering emergent contradictions across those participant voices to mediate and enact organizational change (R. Engeström, 2014).

To demonstrate the potency of knotworking as part of an expansive learning approach, I'll explain what we are doing at my institution. If I had responded to my research findings using a traditional collaborative approach and considering my institutional position as director of writing instruction, I would have formed a university writing committee and convened other members who had institutional authority for writing instruction; for example, the director of FYC. However, knotworking requires a qualitatively different approach. Instead of forming a committee or team, I have been deliberate about creating knotting opportunities, or spaces for ongoing dialogue across stakeholders about our expectations. In sharing my study with colleagues, I have noted the value of simply asking students about their expectations for what student writers need to know and do to be academically proficient writers. I watch for conversations involving multiple stakeholders so that the resulting dialogue can help provide the bridging assistance that Frazier (2010) insisted is necessary to "facilitate transfer outside of FYC" (p. 38). And I have been especially deliberate about asking my colleagues what they think in the presence of students. When the differences emerge (and they always do), I've been making a point of asking, "How did you come to believe x about writing proficiency?" Instead of framing the conversation around what do we do about this problem, I have commented on the differences as interesting and wondered about their implications. As Y. Engeström (2001) framed it, "Contradictions are not the same as problems or conflicts" but "are historically accumulating structural tensions within and between activity systems" (p. 137). Tensions around writing inevitably accrue in a university activity system. Instead of trying to isolate a single problem, I've been encouraging dialogue about our expectations and encouraging participants to say more about why they have them and what the differences might mean. In a knotworking approach to collaboration, this kind of friendly interrogation is necessary and productive (Y. Engeström, 2001).

I have also initiated the idea of developing a shared lexicon, a set of terms that might be useful across the multiple writing contexts in the university. One informal conversation I had recently with a graduate teaching assistant who teaches in our first-year comp program, the director and assistant director of composition in the English department, and another English department member who teaches writing resulted in brainstorming about 15 terms for a shared lexicon. The brainstorming conversation prompted a lively exchange not only on the terms themselves but also about what we believe writing proficiency is and how we have come to hold these beliefs. I wrote down our brainstormed list (on a cocktail napkin) and sent it to them after the confab, and the graduate teaching assistant later drafted and shared her definitions for the terms. Others have added to the list and definitions, and some others, like the assistant director of our writing center, contributed to its refinement. The shared lexicon is now being circulated to writing faculty across campus.

With seemingly mundane mechanisms such as regularly surveying stakeholders' expectations about writing and developing a shared lexicon, I am seeing how our university can enact a knotworking model that also takes advantage of the translational research into practice (TRIP) approach (Smith & Helfenbein, 2009) by providing us a way to easily gather data and translate it into innovative practice faster. Grounded in regular data gathering about expectations, knotworking generates multiple opportunities for coinquiry on writing proficiency that values and uses the expertise of all stakeholders, including the students themselves, rather than relies exclusively on the few designated writing experts on a campus.

That said, I do think we can look to writing program administrators (WPAs) as likely knot initiators. As a WPA, I have learned how to be attuned to emergent matters of concern. Just as I have learned to read student drafts for emergent meaning, I have the capacity to discern and name ideas before they are completely articulated. As a WPA, I am also comfortable with the temporary stability that knotworking fosters. Like drafting, knotworking is my business, and the WPAs on any campus are likely to agree and to embrace this role. At the same time, if we are serious about the horizontal collaboration that knotworking elicits, then we should be very deliberate about ways to invite students, including and perhaps even especially undergraduates, into our knots not only on writing but also on learning generally. Not only would we gain from their contributions but also they would gain more meta-awareness as a result of their role as coinquirers with us as we work to address learning challenges together.

Although I am not proposing that knotworking efforts such as the ones I described are going to result in producing student writers who can repurpose their knowledge of writing across every possible context, they do constitute a point of leverage that could potentially use systems thinking to transform not only writing programs (Melzer, 2013) but also teaching and learning writ large.

Notes

1. I am grateful to my colleague Jeremy Cushman (Western Washington University, Department of English) for his insights in understanding the implications of the knotworking metaphor.

2. Many thanks to my colleague Donna Qualley (Western Washington University, Department of English, director of composition) who facilitated access to these FYC students and instructors in terms of the survey. Donna also did a related study as part of the Elon Research Seminar on Transfer and greatly informed my thinking in both conducting this study and making sense of the results.

References

Engeström, R. (2014). The activity theory approach to learning. *Educational Forum*, *2*(52), 137–146.

Engeström, Y. (2001). Expansive learning at work: Toward an activity-theoretical reconceptualizing. *Journal of Education and Work*, *14*(1), 133–156.

Engeström, Y. (2007). Enriching the theory of expansive learning: Lessons from journeys toward coconfiguration. *Mind, Culture, and Activity*, *14*(1–2), 23–29.

Engeström, Y. (2008). *From teams to knots: Activity-theoretical studies of collaboration and learning at work*. New York, NY: Cambridge University Press.

Engeström, Y., Engeström, M. R., & Vähäaho, T. (1999). When the center does not hold: The importance of knotworking. In S. Chaiklin, M. Hedegaard, & U. J. Jensen (Eds.), *Activity theory and social practice: Cultural–historical approaches* (pp. 345–375). Aarhus, Denmark: Aarhus University Press.

Engeström, Y., & Sannino, A. (2009). Studies of expansive learning: Foundation, findings and future challenges. *Educational Research Review*, *5*, 1–24.

Fraizer, D. (2010). First steps beyond first year: Coaching transfer after FYC. *WPA: Writing Program Administration*, *33*(3), 34–57.

Light, R. J. (2001). *Making the most of college: Students speak their minds.* Cambridge, MA: Harvard University Press.

Melzer, D. (2013). Using systems thinking to transform writing programs. *WPA: Writing Program Administration*, *36*(2), 75–94.

Nowacek, R. (2011). *Agents of integration: Understanding transfer as a rhetorical act.* Carbondale, IL: Southern Illinois University Press.

Smith, J. S., & Helfenbein, R. (2009). Translational research in education: Collaboration and commitment in urban contexts. In W. S. Gershon (Ed.), *The collaborative turn: Working together in qualitative research* (pp. 89–104). Rotterdam, the Netherlands: Sense.

PART TWO

PRINCIPLES AT WORK: IMPLICATIONS FOR PRACTICE CASE STUDIES

8

RETHINKING THE ROLE OF HIGHER EDUCATION IN COLLEGE PREPAREDNESS AND SUCCESS FROM THE PERSPECTIVE OF WRITING TRANSFER

Alison Farrell, Sandra Kane, Cecilia Dube, and Steve Salchak

Impetus for Research

We examine writing transfer across the transition from high school to college at sites in very different national settings: Ireland, South Africa, and the United States. The student profile we discovered of incoming students transitioning from high school to college does not easily match the remediation narrative of disengaged students. Rather, our incoming student profile suggests that the majority of students surveyed in this research are positive about writing, though across incoming cohorts there is a wide range of writing experience and varying levels of familiarity with writing processes. We posit that recognizing what students are bringing to college, which is by no means homogeneous, is essential given the massification of higher education internationally, which has led to greater diversity in the student population. This diversity is never more prevalent than at the point of entry, which still remains for many students a critical moment in the transition from high school to college. Given its significance as a transition point, it is unsurprising that a great deal of research has emerged around the first-year experience and student engagement (Astin, 1984, 1999; Bamber, Trowler, Saunders, & Knight, 2009; Coates, 2006; Harper & Quaye, 2009; Krause & Coates,

2008; Kuh, 2009; Tinto, 2000; Trowler, 2010; Whittaker, 2008; Yorke & Longden, 2008). The magnitude of the transition from high school to college can result in moments of vulnerability for students. In recognition of this fact, many institutions devote significant resources to facilitating the transition of students from these two very different educational settings. Much of this support takes the form of orientation programs and inductions of one sort or another, but more recent research (e.g., Nelson, Smith, & Clarke, 2012) has emphasized the need for a more long-term, multifaceted approach that extends well beyond the first few weeks of college life. Our research supports this view.

Our study focused on writing at this point of transition; specifically, we are interested in transfer and what students bring from writing in high school to college. We suggest that writing transfer at this point of transition is an access issue and that awareness and facilitation of writing transfer could, at individual, departmental, and institutional levels, contribute positively to access agendas. We make this claim because writing is such a significant part of the learning and assessment process for many students in higher education; our contention is that the transition from high school to college, particularly in terms of the access agenda, needs, as a matter of priority, to be mindful of the capacity and necessity of writing transfer for *all* students. Although incoming students from a range of backgrounds (including mature students) bring with them some practices and beliefs that may, in some instances, act as barriers to effective writing, many also display useful processes and positive attitudes to writing that, where acknowledged and built on, could contribute to greater success for students and improved retention for institutions.

Context for Research Project and Research Methods

Though the institutions represented in this case study are in many ways dissimilar, nevertheless, in each location staff and students grapple with the issue of writing transfer at the point of entry to college, both where students are coming directly from high school and where they are arriving in higher education via nontraditional routes. At all three sites there is writing support for students, but the range of services offered, the resources dedicated, and the numbers of students requiring and seeking help vary hugely to the point of being almost incomparable. Yet, despite our differences, all of our sites do exist in a national policy environment of actively promoting broader access to higher education. For the policy goals of enhanced access to be meaningfully achieved, college preparation needs to be conceptualized as an ongoing, active partnership between secondary- and tertiary-level institutions and as a core mission of the university where preparedness is represented as a *process* of transitioning along an education–work continuum. An emphasis on transfer brings sharply into focus the need to provide structured support at and during every transition point across the entire experience. This insight has profound implications for the way we think about college preparation and access. College preparation and access or widening participation programs, which are supportive of effective transfer—including writing transfer—need to consider what happens before, on arrival of, and during the university experience within the broader context of the student's ongoing learning journey.

The three project sites (University of Johannesburg [UJ], South Africa; National University of Ireland, Maynooth [NUI Maynooth]; and George Washington University [GW], United States) vary widely in terms of their local histories regarding issues of access, their entering student populations, and the level of resources available to faculty and students for supporting effective transitions into university writing. Table 8.1 and Table 8.2 offer a snapshot comparison of each site; visit understandingwritingtransfer.com for additional details.

Methodology

To learn more about writing transfer at the transition from high school to college and in the broader context of access to higher education, we addressed two key initial questions:

1. What kinds of writing, processes, and roles are high school and first-year students engaged in (across each of the research sites)?
2. What experiences, knowledge, strategies, and dispositions toward writing and themselves as writers do first-year students bring with them, and how do these attributes help or hinder successful transition to university?

To answer these questions, we used a shared pre- and post-semester student survey to profile writing processes and production in high school and in university, to explore students' attitudes about writing and themselves as writers, to ask students to self-assess their preparedness to write in college, and to consider the impact on their writing and their writing dispositions of the various writing interventions and supports that students might experience in their first year. Given variations in context, the shared survey was localized for institution-specific use, replacing some lexical items with more familiar terms, such as *essay* for *composition* and *marks* for *grades*. The data referred to in this chapter were gathered at the various sites between September 2011 and September 2012. All surveys were distributed in hard copy. At the South

TABLE 8.1
Origins and Enrollment

	University of Johannesburg, South Africa	National University of Ireland, Maynooth	George Washington University, United States
Institution type	Large, comprehensive, urban institution	Autonomous university within National University of Ireland	Private university located in downtown Washington, DC
Established	2005	1997, with origins to the Royal College of St. Patrick (1795)	1824
Enrollment	Approximately 48,000 students, 43,000 of whom are undergraduates	Approximately 9,000 students, all of whom are undergraduates	Approximately 25,000 students, 10,000 of whom are undergraduates
Faculties, colleges, schools	9	3	10
Access demographics	The majority of students (65%) are first generation. English is the second, third, or fourth language of 49.1%. Nearly 33% worry about food, and 60% fear that lack of money will prevent them from graduating.	Maynooth Access Programme[a] (MAP) figures indicate that in 2013–2014, 28% of the full-time undergraduate student population were "nontraditional students," a designation including mature students, students with disabilities, and school leavers from socioeconomic disadvantaged backgrounds.	In the year of the study, 62% of undergraduates were White and 56% were women. The women's leadership program (WLP) cohort involved in this study represents a relatively traditional and privileged student profile: 100% of the WLP cohort are entering university from high school, and 100% of the WLP cohort live together in the dorms.

a. See www.maynoothuniversity.ie/access-office

TABLE 8.2
Support for Writing

University of Johannesburg, South Africa	National University of Ireland, Maynooth	George Washington University, United States
Students on each of the university's four campuses have access to a writing center. No university-wide approach to writing development. No literacy requirement for graduation, and no first-year writing course (or other writing courses), which all students are obliged to take. Academic Development Center offers academic literacies courses to some of the university's 10,000 first-year students on behalf of three of the nine faculties.	The writing center serves all students. No university-wide compulsory writing courses or writing in the discipline courses. There is growing emphasis on oral and written communication skills across the faculties as part of the university's curriculum commission activity and as part of its graduate attributes statement.	All students have access to the university writing center. All incoming students take a four-credit first-year writing course; these courses are capped at a maximum of 17 students per class. To complete their literacy requirement, all students must also take two additional writing-in-the-discipline courses through their majors before graduating.

African site, 470 entering students enrolled in an academic literacies course as part of either their extended degree program in the Faculty of Economics and Financial Sciences (FEFS) or their mainstream studies in the Faculty of Law were surveyed; at the Irish site, 250 entering students enrolled in English as part of an arts degree program were surveyed; and at the American site, 63 entering students enrolled in a first-year women's leadership program were surveyed. In total, 783 students from the three institutions were surveyed.

Key Findings Related to the Essential Principles

Students entering university are generally optimistic and believe in their capacity to learn and to improve as writers. In Ireland, 76% of students either agreed or strongly agreed with the statement "I am a writer"; in South Africa and the United States, the respective percentages were 49% and 67%. When asked about how confident they felt about their ability to write in third level (e.g., higher education or postsecondary education), 84% of American students either agreed or strongly agreed that they felt confident; 72% of Irish students and 71% of South African students felt similarly. In the Irish cohort,

89% of students either agreed or strongly agreed that they enjoyed writing; in the American and South African cohorts, the percentages for this statement were 60.9% and 56%, respectively. When asked about the relevance of writing to their life, South African students responded most positively, with 72% of them declaring writing to be relevant for them. Of American and Irish students, ·67% and 62%, respectively, agreed or strongly agreed with this statement. With particular reference to South African students, the reality on the ground is that many UJ students are underprepared for the demands and rigor of university-level work, particularly in relation to academic writing. Despite this, 71.5% of entering students in 2012 exhibited confidence in their writing capability, and 78% expressed satisfaction with their overall readiness for academic work. Moreover, although many students performed poorly during the year—on both writing assessments and end-of-year grades—by the end of the year, confidence had risen, with over 80% of the research cohort agreeing with the statement "I am confident about my writing." As part of this profile, our data suggest overwhelmingly that students believe that with practice they can become better writers; in Ireland, 90% of students either agreed or strongly agreed that with practice they could become a better writer.

Of the American, Irish, and South African cohorts surveyed, 93%, 84%, and 78%, respectively, had completed six or more short papers (fewer than five pages) in their final year of high school. In regard to longer papers in their final year of second level (e.g., high school or secondary education), 95% of the Irish students had completed one or more longer paper in their final year, 88% of American students had completed one or more longer paper in their final year, and 19% of South African students had completed one or more longer papers in their final year.

It is also worth noting that students in all cohorts typically brought with them the experience of completing some of the sorts of writing forms and assignments that are required in third level. For example, in the Irish institution, 95% of students had experience of writing essays in second level, and 83% and 77% of the cohort had experience of writing answers to questions and narratives (including short stories), respectively. Equally, students brought useful writing processes from second level. At the Irish site, 80% of students brainstormed before writing; 87% sometimes or always revised or proofed; 53% and 43% discussed writing with teacher or another, respectively; 22% had received feedback from another before submitting a piece of writing; and 31% received feedback from teachers before submitting work.

Principle 3: Students' dispositions (e.g., habits of mind) and identities inform the success of their unique writing transfer experiences. Our research suggests, in the first instance, that students *do* bring dispositions and identities to writing in university; writing prior to and in university is not an unbiased activity for them. Data from all three sites strongly suggest that the students surveyed are generally optimistic about writing and enjoy writing. The majority of them are confident about writing, but this confidence does not necessarily translate in either their *perception* of their preparedness or their *actual* preparedness. In terms of writing transfer, the findings reveal a mismatch both positively and negatively between students' dispositions toward writing across all sites and what might be described as their self-efficacy. This is illustrated in the data where, at the beginning of their first year in third level, only 59% of Irish students and 77% of American students felt their second-level courses had prepared them well for writing in university, whereas 78% of South African students felt their second-level experience had prepared them well. The reality in regard to South African students is quite the contrary, resulting in a core "belief" or "dispositional" problem, which is around not a lack of self-esteem but rather overconfidence. Although confidence can be an important attribute and asset, overconfidence can also undermine success. When students have limited awareness about the challenges they are likely to face at the tertiary level and limited self-awareness as writers, they are unlikely to develop useful strategies for effectively dealing with the challenges of university-level work, especially in the absence of structured support. The misalignment between high school for the incoming GW writers, rather than the overconfidence seen in the UJ context, is the shift in writer identity from student to emergent scholar and the discursive, research, and social practices that go along with that transformation.

Associated preparedness difficulties emerge around writing to please and for a grade, which appears to be largely required at second level, versus writing for learning, critical thinking and understanding, inquiry and analysis, meaning-making, or to excel, which is closer to third-level demands. This links closely with the issue of writer identity that is noted in the GW findings and the need to shift from student to emergent scholar. It is reinforced in the mismatch in terms of the processes used in school and those needed in college and a misalignment between students' confidence in writing and their sense of preparedness. The finding of general confidence and enjoyment coupled with a sense of underpreparedness around writing, noted in two of the cohorts, correlates with findings from Scouller, Bonanno, Smith, and Krass (2008), where students reported high self-esteem around writing but low self-efficacy.

Principle 1: Successful writing transfer requires transforming or repurposing prior knowledge (even if only slightly) for a new context to adequately meet the expectations of new audiences and fulfill new purposes of writing. We suggest that to help students transform and repurpose knowledge, we must first better understand what they are bringing to third level in terms of writing processes and writing products; thus, our shared survey profiled student writing experiences in the final year of second level. Results of a survey administered to the UJ lecturers of the students in the study on the kinds of writing (and frequency of writing) done in their classes were also relevant. Findings indicated that students in the study were exposed to more writing and a wider variety of skills in high school than during their first year of study at UJ. Although one lecturer assigned several long pieces of writing a year, the majority assigned between three and six short writing tasks—many involving summarization—and frequently in the form of answers to exam questions. Two courses had no writing component at all. It appears that expectations for writing may not have been sufficiently challenging, which allowed students to conclude that they were well prepared and that their own writing performance was satisfactory.

In NUI Maynooth, the majority of students entering first-year English have completed short and longer written pieces of writing in their final year of second level. In addition, the type of writing that students were completing in second level aligned closely with what they are required to do in first year, which is biased in favor of "answering a specific question" and writing essays. What appears to be lacking, however, is writing in a range of genres at second level, which is reflected in a limited approach to and a *lack of awareness* of genre, purpose, and audience, which students routinely display in the first year in higher education and which leads to their struggling to make the transition from second level to third level. This appears most conspicuously for students in terms of coming to grips with new conventions (e.g., referencing), but it is reflected more obviously for faculty in their struggles around register and structure. This misalignment may contribute to transfer problems, because what students bring to their writing in third level from second level does not align with the new writing demands and is not scaffolded to create a bridge from writing in one arena to writing in another.

In terms of writing processes, there is a great deal of variety and some cause for concern in regard to the mismatch between the kinds of writing processes expected in college and what students have been doing in second level. This suggests that much of the writing processes at the high school level reinforce the high-stakes nature of writing where writing is submitted for review only when a grade is being awarded and that the process of drafting, reviewing, and redrafting is sadly neglected.

In summary, these data suggest that the NUI Maynooth students we surveyed bring the experience of writing for a grade and writing in exams to higher education. They have some experience of writing short pieces and long pieces, but true variety in their writing seems limited. Irish students coming to university have honed some writing processes, including brainstorming, revising, and proofing, and some of them have discussed and received feedback on their writing. In addition, they brought positive attitudes to writing and a belief that they could improve with practice.

In the case of the GW cohort, although there was a slight increase in the amounts of writing done in the first year of college versus the final year of high school, the increase was limited. An examination of the genres written in high school versus those written in college suggested that students' high school writing was also very similar and academically focused, including such commonplace genres as journaling, research papers, timed writing, lab reports, literary analysis, and so on. Motivation and the ways research was conceptualized, though, did vary between high school and college. In high school, GW writers were much more likely to see research as summarizing information or gathering facts, often in support of a preexisting position. They were also much more likely to be motivated by receiving a grade rather than affecting an audience. These are the practices of students. At university, however, GW writers were more likely to experience research as inquiry and as driven by audience needs; they also took a more active and critical posture toward sources and used sources for a greater variety of rhetorical purposes, like constructing a conversation to enter into or as an interpretive lens or as data. These are the practices of emergent scholars.

As a final point, if these high-performing GW writers still struggle with the transition from high school to college writing and need sustained support to manage that transition effectively, it strongly suggests that the ideal of college preparation is deeply problematic in its insistence of a seamless transition; if there is adequate preparation, then there will be in effect no transition. But this is not true. In a new environment, there is always a learning curve.

Principle 4: University programs can "teach for transfer." Enabling practices that promote writing transfer include constructing writing curricula and classes that focus on the study and practice of rhetorically based concepts (e.g., genre, purpose, and audience) that prepare students to analyze expectations for writing and learning within specific contexts, asking students to engage in activities that foster the development of metacognitive awareness, and explicitly modeling transfer-focused thinking. Our data overwhelmingly suggest that students believe that with practice they can become better writers. This belief aligns strongly with the principle that transfer can be taught and has curricular and student support implications. Pedagogically, learning in general, and writing transfer in particular, is much more likely to occur at a deep level where the learning environment is a learner-centered one. Such an environment is mindful of what students are bringing to the process and aims to begin where the students are. In the scenario that our data suggest, where students want to be better writers, believe they can improve through practice, and need to demonstrate this competence through achieving learning goals, it appears that Race's (2012, 2014) central factors that contribute to learning (i.e., needing and wanting) are satisfied. Equally, as our data suggest, students' beliefs in their capacity to learn and to improve as writers does not match the remediation narrative. This suggests that what happens after they get to college is crucial—the university should embrace support upon arrival for all students as a core mission, rather than remediation. This common profile should be recognized, valued, and built on. This has clear implications for offering writing support and for providing opportunities to write. If students are to meet expectations for writing at the higher levels of their university experience, the kind and frequency of writing development provided beforehand is crucial. At UJ, there is no first-year writing requirement, and there are no writing across the curriculum or writing in the discipline programs. The dilemma for UJ, as for universities in many developing countries, is that such initiatives are difficult to implement given the context of large class instruction, which is the norm. Furthermore, many academics resist and feel that "teaching" writing is not their responsibility because of excessive workloads, large student numbers, pressure to get through subject content, time constraints, and lack of expertise (Bharuthram, 2012; Kane, 2013; Seligman & Gravett, 2010).

At the same time, variability across sites suggests a need for tailoring support and for developing approaches that take into account the particular situations of individual campuses and of the internal diversity of entering cohorts. We see variability across sites in terms of the amount and type of school writing that students are doing before entering university, in the expectations for writing once they arrive, and in the misalignments that exist at different sites between the secondary and tertiary levels.

Implications for Policy and Practice

We close with some core implications of this case study for policy and practice.

1. Universities need to recognize that they have an active role to play in transitioning *all* students from high school to college. *All* students benefit from structured support when transitioning from high school to college, though the support that universities provide students must be tailored to address the variable profiles and misalignments of particular cohorts and contexts.

2. Regardless of specific tailoring, interventions need to be sustained and multifaceted, recognize the importance of identity and dispositions for supporting effective transitions, and be sensitized to take better advantage of prior knowledge.
3. To provide effective supports, writing programs and universities more generally need to capture relevant profiles of what students are bringing into their university experience.
4. Writing programs and universities must emphasize the need for initial and continuous professional development support for teachers in higher education, recognizing that good teaching can facilitate effective transfer.
5. Universities globally should recognize that writing programs and writing centers can be important platforms for supporting this kind of transitional work and for promoting the intellectual engagement and retention of students.

Implementing policies that support effective transfer across the critical transition of high school to college will positively affect student engagement and satisfaction, student achievement of learning outcomes, and student retention and can ultimately be a transformative experience for the individual and the institution as a learning organization. To achieve these goals, universities must reinforce the centrality of the learner in the educational experience. It is through this connection with previous knowledge, skills, and strategies that transfer can occur. Universities must also be mindful of the extent to which students' backgrounds, experiences, dispositions, and previous learning affect in a unique way their readiness and capacity to learn from one situation to the next. At an institutional level, the value of what students bring to the learning must be recognized and must provide the foundation for the learning that occurs within the institution. This has significant curricular and pedagogical implications for all students but particularly for those from nontraditional and underrepresented groups. Given this awareness that individual differences and identity do affect transfer, there should be some scope in the curriculum, the pedagogical approaches, and the assessment methods to accommodate a personalization of the learning experience, for example, through personal development planning portfolios, use of learning journals, and a capstone project.

College success is not just about what students bring. It is also about how institutions of higher education recognize and value what they bring and promote effective transfer through instructional designs and institutional supports in the first year and beyond that take identity, dispositions, and other contextual factors into account.

References

Astin, A. W. (1984). Student involvement: A developmental theory for higher education. *Journal of College Student Development, 25*(4), 297–308.

Astin, A. W. (1999). Involvement in learning revisited: Lessons we have learned. *Journal of College Student Development, 40*(5), 587–598.

Bamber, V., Trowler, P., Saunders, M., & Knight, P. (Eds.). (2009). *Enhancing learning and teaching in higher education: Theory, cases, practices.* Buckingham, UK: Open University Press/SRHE.

Bharuthram, S. (2012). Making a case for the teaching of reading across the curriculum in higher education. *South African Journal of Higher Education, 32*(2), 205–214.

Coates, H. C. (2006). *Student engagement in campus-based and online education: University connections.* London, UK: Routledge.

Harper, S. R., & Quaye, S. J. (Eds.). (2009). *Student engagement in higher education.* New York, NY, and London, UK: Routledge.

Kane, S. (2013). Reading and writing in the writing centre: An integrative approach. In *Proceedings of the Higher Education Learning and Teaching Association of Southern Africa (HELTASA) 2012 conference* (pp. 46–54). Pretoria, South Africa: HELTASA.

Krause, K.-L., & Coates, H. (2008). Students' engagement in first-year university. *Assessment and Evaluation in Higher Education, 33*(5), 493–505.

Kuh, G. D. (2009). What student affairs professionals need to know about student engagement. *Journal of College Student Development, 50*(6), 683–706.

Nelson, K. J., Smith, J. E., & Clarke, J. A. (2012). Enhancing the transition of commencing students into university: An institution-wide approach. *Higher Education Research and Development, 31*(2), 185–199.

Race, P. (2012). Updated "ripples model." Retrieved from http://phil-race.co.uk/updated-ripples-model/

Race, P. (2014). *Making learning happen: A guide for post-compulsory education* (3rd ed.). London, UK: Sage.

Scouller, K., Bonanno, H., Smith, L., & Krass, I. (2008). Student experience and tertiary expectations: Factors predicting academic literacy amongst first-year pharmacy students. *Studies in Higher Education, 33*(2), 167–178.

Seligman, J., & Gravett, S. (2010). Literacy development as "a marginalised pedagogical service enterprise" or as a social practice in the disciplines? *Education as Change, 14*(1), 107–120.

Tinto, V. (2000). Taking retention seriously: Rethinking the first year of college. *NACADA Journal, 19*(2), 5–10.

Trowler, V. (2010). *Student engagement literature review.* York, UK: Higher Education Academy. Retrieved from www.heacademy.ac.uk/sites/default/files/studentengagementliteraturereview_1.pdf

Whittaker, R. (2008). *Quality enhancement themes: The first year experience; transition to and during the first year.* Glasgow, Scotland: The Quality Assurance Agency for Higher Education Scotland. Retrieved from http://dera.ioe.ac.uk/11595/1/transition-to-and-during-the-first-year-3.pdf

Yorke, M., & Longden, B. (2008). *The first-year experience of higher education in the UK: Final report.* York, UK: The Higher Education Academy.

9

TEACHING FOR TRANSFER

Liane Robertson and Kara Taczak

As writing transfer researchers have begun to consider how writing knowledge might best transfer between contexts, the question of content becomes increasingly central. This question is particularly essential in the context of first-year composition, for the following reasons: (a) First-year composition represents a critical transition for most students as they cross a threshold between the writing in high school and the writing in college, and (b) first-year composition is a space in which students expect some preparation for the writing they will engage in throughout college and beyond.

Impetus for Research

For decades, programs in first-year composition across the country have included a wide variety of content, none of it creating what we might consider to be a consensus among those teaching composition as to which content is preferable. Content in first-year composition courses across institutions often mirrors that of literature courses, or features content based on media influence and popular culture, builds content around a theme of the instructor's or program's choosing designed for relevance to students. Some content is less defined, as is the case in courses that rely solely on the writing process or on modes of writing to act as content.

As writing studies and transfer scholars, we had many questions about which content would be most effective in first-year composition to help students transfer. What is the relevance of the writing content in first-year composition to writing in other disciplines? What are the expectations of students, faculty (both inside and outside of writing studies), and administrators about the role of first-year composition? Are and are those expectations being met? Most important, could the content in first-year composition be more effective in fostering the transfer of writing knowledge and practices across all the sites of writing students will encounter in college, and, if so, what might that content consist of?

As college writing instructors, we watched as our incoming students transitioned from high school to college and then again from first-year composition to other contexts of writing. Witnessing these critical transitions, we observed that first-year composition was often a site of perceived isolation in which students would perform writing as required for a grade, but they felt that the efforts had no relevance to other courses. This challenge is compounded by the fact that some students enter the first-year composition space with prior knowledge about writing that is often based on the "test-prep" writing that permeates their high school experience. Their beliefs and attitudes about what it means to write "correctly" are based on the test scores, grades, and discourse of assessment common in high school (Scherff & Piazza, 2005). When they transition to college, they often mistakenly assume, especially if they've scored well on standardized tests, that they have already learned to write in high school (Bergmann & Zepernick, 2007; Sommers & Saltz, 2004; Thelin & Taczak, 2013; Tinberg & Nadeau, 2011).

Further complicating this transition, some faculty and administrators see first-year composition as having "universality" in which students prepare for (or attempt to prepare for) writing in other college courses. There is a common assumption both inside and outside of writing studies that first-year composition courses are composed of a "representative" writing, but research and experience indicate writing is not universal (Fulkerson, 2005). This collective expectation that students carry knowledge learned in one context to another or that students "learn to write" in first-year composition and then are expected to write successfully in other disciplines is unrealistic (Bergmann & Zepernick, 2007; Kaufer & Young, 1993). Students often fail to transfer or only partially transfer their writing knowledge to other sites of writing in college for many reasons, one of which is that the content we teach in first-year composition often is not transferable to other contexts.

As instructors, we were interested in finding a way to help students understand that college writing would require something different than high school writing and that they could learn to understand different writing situations but that the writing required wouldn't be the same in every situation. As researchers, we wanted to understand how to help students achieve that transfer, and we understood that the first-year composition content with which we were familiar might not be best suited to that goal.

Context for Research Project and Research Methods

This research involved two separate but parallel studies: a comparison of content across three different sections of first-year composition and a study of the role of reflection in transfer.[1] Both studies took place in 2009–2010 at a Research 1 university, within a large first-year composition program with courses ranging widely in content and delivered by graduate teaching assistants. The program featured a selection of strands from which instructors could choose, as well as a number of courses with a variety of themes as developed by individual instructors.

Study participants were recruited from sections of the second sequence of the two required first-year composition courses at this university, which featured students who had placed directly into the second course in the sequence with an appropriate test score or had completed the first course in the sequence before arriving, either at high school or at a community college. Participants were studied during the fall semester while enrolled in the first-year composition course and during the spring semester as they took a variety of courses across the university. Seven individuals participated in the content-comparison study, and six took part in the reflection study.

A number of methods were used in both studies: (a) student interviews, (b) analysis of student writing, (c) analysis of course materials, and (d) instructor interviews and instructor journals. Each study used these methods in exploring student writing within the context of first-year composition during the first semester of the study; in the second semester of the study, student writing in a range of other courses with the context of the social sciences, humanities, and sciences was explored.

Although the studies were conducted separately, they shared a key element: Students from both studies were enrolled in a first-year composition section that featured as its content a *teaching for transfer* (TFT) design, explained next. All six participants in the reflection study were enrolled in the TFT-designed course for first-year composition. Of the seven total participants in the content comparison study, three were enrolled in the TFT course, two in a course with an expressivist design, and two in a course that focused on media and culture as its content.

Key Findings Related to the Essential Principles

The question of the content most effective for transfer of writing knowledge and practice is essential to our work in the classroom and to the development of writing courses in the future. The research indicates that content designed to transfer is critical to student success in writing.

Transfer of First-Year Composition Content

If we want students to transfer what they know about writing to new contexts, they must be able to understand that all writing is situational and that expectations for writing situations must be abstracted before writing *in* those situations can be successful. In other words, students must understand which knowledge to reference and which practices to employ in every situation; they need to be able to frame different writing situations to write effectively in them. This challenge is what first-year composition students must face, but course content in anything other than writing diminishes successful transfer.

Much of the recent research in writing transfer has suggested that content is critical in fostering successful transfer (Brent, 2012; Dew, 2003; Downs & Wardle, 2007; Nowacek, 2011; Yancey, Robertson, & Taczak, 2014), with most researchers arguing that content about writing should be the focus of first-year composition. Research has demonstrated that themed courses do little to encourage transfer because students tend to focus on the theme rather than on learning about writing (Yancey et al., 2014). Students who complete a first-year composition course that lacks discernible content often revert back to what they learned in high school in later contexts that require a different writing approach (Jarratt, Mack, Sartor, & Watson, 2007). Without an understanding of writing concepts and without the vocabulary needed to articulate ideas about writing, students are unable to find success in other contexts (Hilgers, Hussey, & Stitt-Bergh, 1999; Jarratt et al., 2007). These problems contribute to a failure to transfer from first-year composition to other writing contexts.

Content that will transfer, therefore, requires that we accommodate the prior knowledge that students bring into first-year composition; it requires that we provide students with content about writing that they can define and grapple with and later discern; it requires that they develop a conceptual framework of writing knowledge (Beaufort, 2007) that can be repurposed in new contexts; and it requires that they develop a reflective framework for thinking about writing in ways that allow them to achieve transfer. In other words, successful transfer requires curricula deliberately designed for transfer. One such curricular design follows.

Teaching for Transfer in First-Year Composition: Writing Concepts and a Reflective Framework

The TFT course outlined next is designed to encourage students to become *active agents* (as defined by Yancey, 1998) in the development of their own ability to transfer. Although many transfer scholars agree that transfer can be successful, we must be explicit in our teaching for transfer to occur. TFT requires a commitment to transfer as the ultimate outcome of teaching.

The content of the TFT course is composed of three *j*
ponents: writing concepts or *key terms*, the use of a *refle*
framework for thinking about writing concepts and prac
development of a *theory of writing* as an underlying, reiterative *a*
feature that culminates in an end-of-semester articulation of the knowleag_
gained and practices engaged in, including an analysis of the situations for
which rhetorical choices were made. This represents the conceptual framework advocated by Beaufort (2007) and enables students to theorize future
contexts for writing in which the knowledge they now have can be expected
to transfer.

The first component of the course (key terms) provides a foundation
that guides everything from the readings to the class activities and the major
assignments. Eight key terms that we believe students need to understand
for success in other writing situations are introduced, modeled, and reiter-
ated within multiple assignments; they include *rhetorical situation/exigence,
audience, genre, reflection, knowledge, context, discourse community*, and *purpose*. The second component of the course (reflection) focuses on three
types of reflective practice: reflective theory, reflective activities, and reflective assignments. Reflection is used in explicit and intentional ways to help
aid students in understanding both their identity as a writer and the creation of their theory of writing. The third component (theory of writing) is
a reflective process over the course duration that asks students to explore
their relationships with writing: their writing processes, their understanding of key terms they enact in their own writing, and their ability to create
a knowledge base of writing and its practices. Students use this conceptual
knowledge from the course and other writing experiences to inform their
theory of writing.

Prior Knowledge, Themed Courses, and the Myth of Process

Our research illustrated that key terms or writing concepts helped students get past the barriers to learning that their own prior knowledge created (Bransford, Pellegrino, & Donovan, 2000; Driscoll & Wells, 2012;
Robertson, Taczak, & Yancey, 2012). Students who took the TFT course
experienced challenges that acted as catalysts for moving beyond their prior
experiences to a point where they saw themselves as novice writers in college and thus became open to new concepts, allowing the prior knowledge
that was holding them back to be released. Conversely, students who took
a themed course or had content based in literature or popular culture were
more resistant to releasing any prior knowledge that acted as a barrier to
new ideas about writing. Rather than identifying as novices, which according
to Sommers and Saltz (2004) would allow them to more successfully move

.oward expertise in writing at college (Bransford et al., 2000; Carter, 1990), they saw themselves as having mastered college writing and were therefore unwilling to take up new ideas about writing. For some of these students, this ultimately led to disappointing results or even failure in other contexts of writing as they transferred inappropriately to the new situation.

The TFT course's three components—key terms, reflection, and students' theory of writing—serve as means of bridging prior knowledge about writing to the new knowledge students are learning to increase successful transfer. Together, the course components help students create an understanding of writing within the context of college and an awareness of their writing identity, important for transfer because students most often identify not as writers but rather as students who occasionally have to write for class. By establishing identities as writers, they can begin to understand their stance as novice writers, thereby "writing their way into expertise" (Sommers & Saltz, 2004) and increasing their chances of successful transfer.

The TFT curriculum aligns with the conceptual model that Beaufort (2007) advocated, contributing the *subject-matter knowledge* that represents one of her five knowledge domains. The importance of subject-matter knowledge is evidenced in our research as well, with participants in the TFT course demonstrating an understanding about writing as both subject matter and activity (Adler-Kassner & Wardle, 2015). Other participants could not discern writing content from themed content; they were therefore unable to develop the subject-matter knowledge Beaufort (2007) called for. These participants engaged in writing strategies and significant process writing but did not study writing as the TFT participants had and thus only transferred writing practices but did not develop the conceptual framework to transfer to contexts beyond the first-year composition course. For example, one participant reported that he failed a writing assignment in another course because he had unsuccessfully applied the expressive writing he had learned in first-year composition to a theoretical analysis. This failure prompted his understanding of the difference in writing contexts that students in the TFT course had explored.

For all participants, the practice of writing was no substitute for the subject-matter knowledge, as Beaufort (2007) suggested. A mistaken belief in composition studies, as Kaufer and Young (1993) pointed out, is that *doing writing* is what matters and that writing about any subject will suffice, but our participants proved otherwise. Participants who experienced a theme or indiscernible content were unable to make connections across assignments or articulate the purpose of writing in different ways. For example, a participant in the media/culture first-year composition course perceived that the purpose of his research essay assignment was to review an artist he was profiling rather than to demonstrate the incorporation of evidence into writing, as the instructor intended. This lack of understanding was due in part to the previously mentioned focus on the theme of a course as its content; this participant perceived the theme as subject matter.

Reflection is a critical part of the content of the TFT course; we should clarify that although reflection is practiced in many first-year composition courses, the reflective framework of the TFT course is more intricate than reflecting on one's writing as part of the process. In the TFT course, reflection is reiterative so it helps make connections between writing contexts; reflection is systematic so it both involves and is shaped by the conceptual framework students are developing; and reflection is explicit and deliberate so it "arouses mindfulness" and encourages "active self-monitoring," two of the conditions that Perkins and Salomon (1992) suggested are necessary for transfer. By using reflection in these ways, the TFT course creates an environment in which students not only learn but also think about their learning in critical and mindful ways, making reflection the means by which students learn to define and frame (and often reframe) their knowledge for successful transfer (Yancey et al., 2014).

In our research, we found that participants used reflection in specific ways that helped them connect writing situations and transfer writing knowledge between each context. First, the reflection practiced in the TFT course became integrated into the writing process for most of the participants, who found value in looking backward at their writing so they could move forward to the next writing assignment, making connections between past and present and identifying elements that could carry over. Second, as students developed their "theory of writing" in the TFT course, they did so reiteratively, learning in the process not only to frame but also to reframe each new writing situation according to expectations and centered on their current theory of writing, an intellectual practice they continued on their own and transferred beyond the first-year composition course to other contexts. Finally, reflection can provide a vehicle for successful transfer if it is taught intentionally for transfer, as explained earlier. Participants found that their theory of writing and the key terms they incorporated into that theory were what they reflected on in looking back at their writing and what they looked for in new writing situations. The key terms and theory of writing enabled them to transfer writing knowledge and practice via the reflective framework developed in the TFT course (Yancey et al., 2014).

Implications for Curricular Design: Teaching for Transfer

As the research on prior knowledge and dispositions has indicated, there is much that students must overcome in learning to write successfully in college. In high school there is often pressure for students to be exempted from first-year composition courses, but successful exemption can create a false sense of expertise (Sommers & Saltz, 2004) that doesn't always serve those students well when they write in college courses; students who take first-year composition courses outside of the college environment or who opt out are often at a disadvantage in the long term for writing effectively at the college level (Jolliffe & Phelan, 2006). This idea is perpetuated by college writing courses that are similar in content to high school writing and by the perception that first-year composition isn't preparing students for the kind of writing expected in other disciplines. A curriculum that teaches for transfer in first-year composition would counter these notions by better preparing students for various writing contexts.

One of the key factors in the success of the TFT model is that transfer is an explicit goal of the course, articulated often by the instructor and discussed at length in the classroom. Students in the course are able to identify which knowledge they might apply to another context in part because they understand the learning objective is to transfer, so they actively seek the opportunity to transfer or recognize when they have transferred. Participants in other types of first-year composition courses who are not engaged in the reiterative and substantive reflection of the TFT course might engage in serendipitous transfer, but they are not able to replicate it in other contexts where needed.

As we suggested earlier, TFT requires a commitment to transfer as the ultimate outcome of teaching. It would require that first-year composition programs and instructors agree to make the development of students' ability to transfer writing knowledge and practices across contexts a priority. The example we provided here, the TFT course, was based on our research but also on our beliefs as scholars in rhetoric and composition and on our extensive study and work in this area. It was not a difficult course for us to teach given our background, but it may be so for instructors with experience in other areas of English, and it may not be accepted as easily by those who would prefer to teach writing courses according to their strengths and interests. But if transfer is the goal of teaching in all disciplines, then it should also be the goal of first-year composition. The challenges for programs and instructors are significant to put this type of content into our classrooms but are outweighed by the benefits to students who seek success as college writers. While research on writing transfer continues, the question of content in first-year composition remains. If our ultimate aim in every writing course is transfer, students can become more successful writers in and beyond college.

Note

1. These studies were first reported in Liane Robertson's (2011) *The Significance of Course Content in the Transfer of Writing Knowledge From First-Year Composition to Other Academic Writing Contexts* and Kara Taczak's (2011) *Connecting the Dots: Does Reflection Foster Transfer?* and are further detailed in *Writing Across Contexts: Transfer, Composition, and Sites of Writing* (Yancey et al., 2014).

References

Adler-Kassner, L., & Wardle, E. (Eds.). (2015). *Naming what we know: Threshold concepts in writing studies*. Logan, UT: Utah State University Press.

Beaufort, A. (2007). *College writing and beyond: A new framework for university writing instruction*. Logan, UT: Utah State University Press.

Bergmann, L. S., & Zepernick, J. S. (2007). Disciplinarity and transference: Students' perceptions of learning to write. *WPA: Writing Program Administration, 31*(1–2), 124–149.

Bransford, J. D., Pellegrino, J. W., & Donovan, M. S. (Eds.). (2000). *How people learn: Brain, mind, experience, and school* (Expanded ed., pp. 31–50). Washington, DC: National Academies Press.

Brent, D. (2012). Crossing boundaries: Co-op students relearning to write. *College Composition and Communication, 63*(4), 558–592.

Carter, M. (1990). The idea of expertise: An exploration of cognitive and social dimensions of writing. *College Composition and Communication, 41*(3), 265–286.

Dew, D. F. (2003). Language matters: Rhetoric and writing I as content course. *WPA: Writing Program Administration, 26*(3), 87–104.

Downs, D., & Wardle, E. (2007). Teaching about writing, righting misconceptions: (Re)envisioning "first-year composition" as "introduction to writing studies." *College Composition and Communication, 58*(4), 552–584.

Driscoll, D. L., & Wells, J. H. M. (2012). Beyond knowledge and skills: Writing transfer and the role of student dispositions. *Composition Forum, 26*, 1–15.

Fulkerson, R. (2005). Composition at the turn of the twenty-first century. *College Composition and Communication, 56*(4), 654–687.

Hilgers, T., Hussey, E., & Stitt-Bergh, M. (1999). As you're writing you have these epiphanies. *Written Communication, 16*(3), 317–353.

Jarratt, S. C., Mack, K., Sartor, A., & Watson, S. E. (2007). *Pedagogical memory and the transferability of writing knowledge: An interview-based study of UCI juniors and seniors*. Unpublished manuscript, University of California.

Jolliffe, D. A., & Phelan, B. (2006). Advanced placement, not advanced exemption: Challenges for high schools, colleges, and universities. In K. B. Yancey (Ed.), *Delivering college composition: The fifth canon* (pp. 89–103). Portsmouth, NH: Boynton/Cook.

102 PRINCIPLES AT WORK

Kaufer, D., & Young, R. (1993). Writing in the content areas: Some theoretical complexities. In L. Odell (Ed.), *Theory and practice in the teaching of writing: Rethinking the discipline* (pp. 71–104). Carbondale, IL: Southern Illinois University Press.

Nowacek, R. S. (2011). *Agents of integration: Understanding transfer as a rhetorical act.* Carbondale and Edwardsville, IL: Southern Illinois University Press.

Perkins, D. N., & Salomon, G. (1992). Transfer of learning. In T. N. Postlethwaite & T. Husen (Eds.), *International encyclopedia of education* (2nd ed., pp. 2–13). Oxford, UK: Pergamon.

Robertson, L. (2011). *The significance of course content in the transfer of writing knowledge from first-year composition to other academic writing contexts* (Doctoral dissertation). Florida State University, Tallahassee, FL.

Robertson, L., Taczak, K., & Yancey, K. B. (2012). Notes toward a theory of prior knowledge and its role in college composers' transfer of knowledge and practice. *Composition Forum, 26.* Retrieved from http://compositionforum.com/issue/26/prior-knowledge-transfer.php

Scherff, L., & Piazza, C. (2005). The more things change, the more they stay the same: A survey of high school students' writing experiences. *Research in the Teaching of English, 39*(3), 271–304.

Sommers, N., & Saltz, L. (2004). The novice as expert: Writing the freshman year. *College Composition and Communication, 56,* 124–149.

Taczak, K. (2011). *Connecting the dots: Does reflection foster transfer?* (Doctoral dissertation). Florida State University, Tallahassee, FL.

Thelin, W. H., & Taczak, K. (2013). (Re)envisioning the divide: Juliet five years later. *Teaching English in the Two-Year College, 41*(1), 6–19.

Tinberg, H., & Nadeau, J. P. (2011). Contesting the space between high school and college in the era of dual-enrollment. *College Composition and Communication, 62*(4), 704–725.

Yancey, K. B. (1998). *Reflection in the writing classroom.* Logan, UT: Utah State University Press.

Yancey, K. B., Robertson, L., & Taczak, K. (2014). *Writing across contexts: Transfer, composition, and sites of writing.* Logan, UT: Utah State University Press.

STUDENT DRAFTING BEHAVIORS IN AND BEYOND THE FIRST-YEAR SEMINAR

Diane E. Boyd

Impetus for Research

In 2008, Furman University (a small, private, liberal arts college in the southern United States) adopted its first curriculum revision in over 40 years, incorporating an "intellectually-incendiary" first-year writing (FYW) program in which one of two courses in the sequence is writing intensive (Curriculum Review Committee, 2005, p. 9). Faculty from across the disciplines teach FYWs, a challenge that invites those not trained in composition to teach outside their comfort zones; accordingly, direct instruction regarding rhetorical purpose, audience, and strategies varies widely from one course to another. Despite the obvious challenge of teaching first-year composition with minimal training, more than 50% of the faculty reported a "high level of satisfaction" with the program and its goals. We had been moderately successful, but with accreditation visits looming, we had more work to do.

Previous research at our institution indicated that students made moderate gains in writing proficiency in the FYWs, but little to no progress was made in the middle drafting stages (Kolb, Longest, & Jensen, 2012). These findings, our context, and our continued campus conversation about the "value" of the first-year seminar program stimulated my research questions. Given that over half of FYW faculty had not been trained to teach composition, could one small teaching tweak bolster student effort during the drafting stage? Might one small drafting step (in this case, the reverse outline) improve student persistence in "stuck places"? Is there a correlation between persistence and developing a writerly identity? Finally, will these writing skills and dispositions transfer beyond the first year and into upper-division writing tasks? My role as faculty developer provides a unique position from which to research these questions, not simply through the usual avenues of consultations and workshops with faculty but through orchestrating multi-class Scholarship of Teaching and Learning (SoTL) research. If students showed moderate improvements using the reverse outline protocol, I could then work with our writing program administrator/first-year experience coordinator to fold it into our faculty development workshops and in my consultations with faculty on their assignment design. Eventually the findings could inform how we develop and measure learning outcomes for the FYWs.

Contexts for Research Project and Research Methods

Previous qualitative interviews of Furman University first-year students revealed that student writers typically expend energy and attention at the initial and final stages of the writing process (prewriting and revision) but devote less time, energy, and attention to the middle stages (planning and drafting) (Kolb et al., 2012). In their work, Kolb and colleagues identified a spectrum of drafting behaviors, from no drafting (writing an essay in one sitting) to intentional redrafting while the document is still private (prior to peer feedback or evaluation). Kolb and colleagues' data show that "although most students improve their planning and revising strategies, few made noticeable gains in their prewriting and drafting activities. During their interviews, students described investing heavily in the very beginning and at the very end of the writing process" (Kolb et al., 2012, p. 27). These surprising findings run counter to most writing process research, a fact that may be explained by the academically talented, potentially fixed mind-set of many Furman students. Fixed mind-set students are driven by earning As, thus it makes sense that student motivation would be high early and late in the writing process, especially when that process is attached to a product that will be submitted for a grade (Dweck, 2006). Kolb and colleagues' study showed that student writing energy and proficiency in the middle stages (or "struggle stages," where attention and energy to the writing task flag) improved little as a result of students' FYW experience. Kolb and colleagues theorized that building an additional "assignment step" during the middle stages might help amplify students' attention to this point in the process.

My two-phase study builds directly on this prior research.[1] In the first phase, 14 faculty (6 in the English department) teaching in our FYW program agreed to include a common intervention: the reverse outline. In this process, students outline their essays after they compose them to determine where they might need to restructure, reshape, or completely overhaul their writing or ideas. Our particular protocol asked students to consider these questions with each paragraph: *What is the purpose of this paragraph? What is this paragraph accomplishing? What does this paragraph contribute to the argument?* After completing the reverse outline, students considered the following reflective questions:

1. What issue, problem, or question does this essay address, and how does it respond?
2. Describe the audience to whom the essay is addressed.
3. What needs to be moved to better establish a logical sequence?
4. If you had more time to work on the draft, what would you add, delete, or change?

A consensus among faculty about the intervention type and wording of the reflective questions was reached over the course of two focus group meetings. We selected a single intervention (the reverse outline) for study uniformity, but the group also acknowledged that any drafting step that prompts students to think metacognitively could be beneficial. Writing journals, writing reflective prompts on the writing process (rather than anchored in the text), and writing questionnaires were other options we considered.

There was variation in how faculty used the reverse outline process: Some used it in or prior to peer review; others had students respond to the questions in writing. Each colleague participating agreed to use the process at least one time after the semester's first writing assignment.

Although there are a number of ways to stimulate metacognitive thinking in novice writers (e.g., see Robertson & Taczak, this volume), the reverse outline protocol is particularly powerful because it often illuminates for students *what is missing* logically or rhetorically (King, 2012). It encourages them to consider moving things around, one of the behaviors that distinguishes novice writers from expert ones. Because writers must pause to consider their own writing during the reverse outline process, using the four metacognitive questions described previously, we considered it a drafting strategy that could potentially strengthen the writing process and have implications for transfer.

In the second phase of the study, sophomore students completed in-depth follow-up interviews to discuss their writing process with text in hand. Students were again asked to describe their writing process and point to "stuck places" in their drafts, delineating their methods for working through the bottlenecks.

Key Findings Related to the Essential Principles

Although 15 weeks is a short time to make appreciable gains, qualitative assessment of pre- and postintervention interviews indicate a modest increase in drafting behaviors over the course of the semester (we achieved statistical significance where p = .0001). Most interviewees did not mention the reverse outline in their posttreatment interviews, which is instructive on two counts, both of which are related to the key principles this volume illustrates. First, it could mean that student writers saw the reverse outline as organic to the composition and transfer process, which aligns with Principle 1 (successful writing transfer requires transforming or repurposing prior knowledge). Second, students repurposed prior knowledge (the activity of completing the reverse outline) into other strategies for working through writing stuck places. The reverse outline was just one more strategy students used to persist.

We measured persistence in terms of the number and variety of "bottleneck strategies"—the deliberate activities students called on when they got stuck while writing. These strategies ranged from the quotidian to the ritualistic (taking yoga breaks, going for a walk, using eye drops, listening to music in another language). These behaviors promote physical or environmental changes that "reset" the writer for the task; although they have their place in a repertoire of bottleneck strategies, they aren't cognitive in nature and therefore don't force students to new understandings of their writing process or of themselves as writers.

Other more cognitive bottleneck strategies also came into play. In first-round interviews, 19 of 25 students relied primarily on filling in the gaps of an outline to generate a draft, an organizational metacognitive step. Kelly remembered generating four outlines for the paper she discussed, describing their transformation from list to prose this way: "Yeah, it starts off kind of blocky and then you add things and slowly my outline can turn into full paragraphs. And then, once I get that far, I can, you know, start to finish it all up. Delete all the Roman numerals and insert a few transitional sentences and then it starts to work as a paper." Reliance on a premade outline or thought map *increased* in second-round interviews: 22 of 25 students reported filling in the gaps to some extent at their follow-up interviews. Outlines (written or mental) reduce attentional overload and, in the case of one experiment, improved writing quality (Kellogg, 1988). Although filling in gaps helps students manage the cognitive load, it deliberately reduces the amount of information students are mentally juggling as they compose and thus decreases the perceived effort in the "struggle stage" of writing, which proves an effective strategy for novice writers.

At the conclusion of each interview, students were asked which part of the writing process they enjoyed most. Most reported completing the essay; the passionate release with which they described finishing was surprising. Yuqi confessed, "Finishing it . . . it's such a relief. Because I was really stressed out and it feels like my heart is tight or something. And I just . . . everything is . . . constricted!" It's as if the act of procrastination and then writing under time pressure generated physical pain in students, and there was little recognition that much of that pain is self-inflicted. In fact, Logan reported writing a draft in one sitting as a kind of service to the reader:

> The whole paper, for me, has to be a train of thought from top to bottom and so . . . it helps me to be able to write it all in one sitting so that it reads like . . . because someone is going to read it in one sitting, probably, so if they're reading it all in one sitting, it feels more jumpy usually if you write it at different times because your mind is in a different place . . . so I try to keep that in mind because it helps the reader, I think, too.

Logan's complex rationalization of a "one and done" drafting approach is evidence that he has the ability to juggle multiple perspectives or ideas (as we do when we write), rationalizing that it's increased audience awareness that compels him to write in a single sitting. Like other students proficient at articulating a coherent argument in a first draft, he simply doesn't see the need to write multiple drafts. Academically talented students prefer the self-inflicted, familiar pain of procrastination to the less familiar discomfort of confronting stuck places in their writing. It is common for novice writers to impose time constraints on themselves, but this research illuminates that this tactic—procrastination—prevents students not only from getting stuck but also from learning what to do when they get stuck (develop bottleneck strategies). In other words, their proficiency as novice, one-draft writers prevents them from developing the persistence that could engender a more writerly identity.

This finding (in both its negative and its positive valences) supports Principle 3 (students' dispositions and identities inform the success of their unique writing transfer experiences). To build new identities as writers, students must struggle through mystifying stuck places or bottlenecks just prior to a threshold experience. Typically, novice writers will retreat when they face these stuck places, or, as my research found, they avoid confronting them altogether by compressing the drafting timeline to a single sitting.

The research showed a subtle shift in student persistence between the fall and the spring semesters, however. With the work of one semester behind them, students arrived in the spring FYW mentally tired, but the cumulative

Figure 10.1. Average increase of bottleneck strategies in pre- and postinterviews.

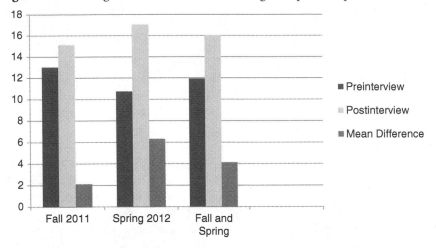

effort of academic life up to that point helped them use more and different bottleneck strategies than their fall semester FYW counterparts (see Figure 10.1).

There was more evidence that students continued to remix their bottleneck strategies, and thus develop a more writerly identity, in the sophomore year follow-up interviews. Students brought along a recent essay, described the writing process for that sample, and located a sticking point in the drafting process, explaining how they worked through it. Five of 25 students returned in their sophomore year, but those who did participate could more effectively articulate their process *even as* they continued to grapple with their identities as writers.

Two of these five students indicated that properly addressing counterarguments (without allowing them to overshadow their own theses) was difficult. Their bottleneck strategies included going back to their own words and refining their position, as well as building in adequate time to think about the complexities of their hypotheses (rather than waiting until the last minute to attempt the draft). Melissa discussed forming a writing group as a way to work through stuck places during her sophomore interview. She recalled with relish working late hours in campus classrooms; her enthusiasm for the effort was unmistakable. These bottleneck strategies (self-regulating time on a thinking task, retracing the steps of the argument, forming feedback networks) require participants to self-regulate and engage in metacognition in ways that the first-year "reset" strategies do not.

Rather than step away and reset as they had in the previous year, students in their second year were more persistent and managed their writing load more successfully, identifying "the moment when the thinking comes together" after concerted effort as a predominant "favorite" part of the process. Kevin summed up his favorite part of the process, not as "getting it done" but as "knowing what I want to say, and seeing those thoughts complete." Another student remarked that stuck places "jumped out" at him during drafting, and working through these bottlenecks allowed him to see more clearly the "connections to other courses." Students remixed elements of the reverse outline (specifically the metacognitive steps inherent in reflection) to ask themselves questions and persist through stuck places, developing "new ways of thinking about how to write and about what writing is" (Robertson, Taczak, & Yancey, 2012).

Sophomore writers discussed the process with more nuance, included more pauses to collect thought, and enjoyed more good-humored laughter than they did during their tension-filled first-year interviews. In other words, sophomore students were poised on the threshold of new conceptions of themselves as writers. These findings align with threshold concepts theory in that this new way of knowing engenders "a transfiguration of identity and adoption of an extended or elaborated discourse" (Meyer & Land, 2005, p. 21). In describing their writing process, second-year students used more dynamic language, signaling a shift not only in their writing activities but also in their conceptions of themselves as active agents in the writing process: Writing is something you *do*, not something *done to you*. Thus, the study foregrounds the interplay between behaviors and identity; student identity and dispositions, perhaps more than strategies or behaviors, are key elements in promoting persistence and amplifying student writing efficacy in FYW courses and beyond. Developing habits or behavior can help students along in their development of writerly identities.

Modeling the practice of using a metacognitive drafting strategy (the reverse outline) helped students creatively remix their own signature bottleneck strategies as they became more experienced writers. The study was designed with the hope that students would reuse the reverse outline in future writing tasks in a kind of low-road transfer. Instead, sophomore-year interviews showed students repurposing the reverse outline by developing signature bottleneck strategies in a developmentally appropriate far transfer: Because sophomore students are "new" in their disciplines, their early writing within that discipline will necessarily seem "vastly different from" their previous "context for learning" (Perkins & Salomon, 1992). The reverse outline helped novice writers gain the confidence to develop multiple and more effective signature bottleneck strategies, which indicates the development of an inchoate expert writerly identity.

Implications for Curriculum Design

Our faculty and administrators built the first-year seminar program on the tacit belief that the writing skills learned in the FYW seminar would transfer to upper-division courses and professional contexts; in retrospect, expecting these results from faculty who had yet to receive adequate development opportunities might have been overly optimistic. This research showed that student persistence, and thus students' conception of themselves as writers, is positively affected by the addition of a single metacognitive drafting step. In this study, we hypothesized that the behavior might build the mind-set, a kind of improvisation that is not foreign to expert writers (who have signature bottleneck strategies or writing rituals of their own) but that may be uncomfortable to novice writers who view themselves, at times, as passive victims of the writing tasks they are assigned.

At Furman, we've begun including the reverse outline and other metacognitive writing activities in our FYW faculty workshops and helped faculty redesign assignments to include such steps. Because learning to write produces heavy cognitive load, we coach colleagues to decrease academically incendiary content and build in time for direct writing instruction. Our next priority is to help faculty "teach for transfer": coaching students to "a robust understanding of (the) underlying principles" (Ambrose, Bridges, DiPietro, Lovett, & Norman, 2010, p. 108) at work in writing skills and behavior. We are revising our assessment plan of the FYW program to factor in expectations for student writing that extend beyond measuring products and include evaluating the processes or experiences students navigate in the FYW.

More broadly, our institution is in the midst of a curriculum-changing discussion about the measurable impact of the FYW program; because of the program's instructional expense, some administrators and faculty support truncating the first-year seminar program experience from two courses to one. We are exploring two very different responses to this question, both of which could be supported by this research. Because drafting behaviors increased more in the spring semester FYW than in the fall semester FYW, one solution may be a deliberate sequence in which students complete the nonwriting first-year seminar in the fall semester and the FYW during the spring semester. An alternative (one that would require further curriculum revision) would be to require a single FYW and a writing-intensive course in the sophomore year after students have selected a disciplinary focus. Although this research has been shared with administrators and disseminated at faculty retreat sessions, our FYW program continues to consider how we might revise or restructure the FYW program to maximize our instructional resources and amplify student learning.

This research, or iterations of it, could inform research or decision-making processes at other institutions with various contexts. First-year experience administrators and faculty oversight committees might reframe how they implement curriculum shifts with more explicit attention to teaching for transfer, with an emphasis on helping students through the laborious "middle stages" of writing with metacognitive bottleneck strategies. The framing research questions could be repurposed into a campus-appropriate inquiry, such as the following: How do students who struggle with writing more generally approach bottlenecks? To what degree does a metacognitive drafting step help students construct a sense of themselves as writers? How do we help faculty work through the stuck places of teaching writing?

Growth-mind-set guru Carol S. Dweck (2006) urged learners to focus on portions of tasks (or, in this case, portions of an FYW program) that aren't meeting full potential. In this spirit, we seek to employ tactical thinking about our FYW program's situational factors and learner context. The primary research question ("What one small teaching tweak can improve student writing?") led to intriguing evidence about how academically talented novice writers use metacognitive drafting strategies and the extent to which they embrace more writerly identities. Leadership teams in a variety of contexts might repurpose the theory behind this research. When professors and administrators shift their understanding of student writing from a "performance of a set of skills" toward "a process that yields an identity cultivated over time," the ways we assess writing proficiency will become more rich and instructive. Assisting faculty and students to confront their "stuck places"—in teaching, writing, and life—may be one of this project's most empowering, transferrable results.

Note

1. This research was supported by the Elon research seminar on Writing Transfer and the First-Year Seminar Committee at Furman University. The author would like to thank Mike Winiski, who provided statistical analysis, and Furman student coresearchers Lacey Brantley (2013) and Sonya Joseph (2015).

References

Ambrose, S. A., Bridges, M. W., DiPietro, M., Lovett, M. C., & Norman, M. K. (2010). *How learning works: Seven research-based principles for smart teaching*. San Francisco, CA: Jossey-Bass.

Curriculum Review Committee. (2005). *Invigorating intellectual life: A proposal for Furman University's academic program and calendar.* Greenville, SC: Furman University.

Dweck, C. (2006). *Mindset: The new psychology of success.* New York, NY: Random House.

Kellogg, R. T. (1988). Attentional overload and writing performance: Effects of rough draft and outline strategies. *Journal of Experimental Psychology: Learning, Memory, and Cognition, 14*(2), 355–365. doi:10.1037/0278-7393.14.2.355

King, C. L. (2012). Reverse outlining: A method for effective revision of document structure. *IEEE Transactions on Professional Communication, 55*(3), 254–261.

Kolb, K. H., Longest, K. C., & Jensen, M. J. (2012). Assessing the writing process: Do writing-intensive first-year seminars change how students write? *Teaching Sociology, 41*(1), 20–31. doi:10.1177/0092055X12448777

Meyer, J. H. F., & Land, R. (2005). Introduction. In J. H. F. Meyer & R. Land (Eds.), *Overcoming barriers to student understanding: Threshold concepts and troublesome knowledge* (pp. 3–18). London, UK: Routledge.

Perkins, D. N., & Salomon, G. (1992). The science and art of transfer. *If Minds Matter: A Foreword to the Future, 1,* 201–210.

Robertson, L., Taczak, K., & Yancey, K. B. (2012). Notes toward a theory of prior knowledge and its role in college composers' transfer of knowledge and practice. *Composition Forum, 26.* Retrieved from http://compositionforum.com/issue/26/prior-knowledge-transfer.php

11

CUEING AND ADAPTING FIRST-YEAR WRITING KNOWLEDGE

Support for Transfer Into Disciplinary Writing

Gwen Gorzelsky, Carol Hayes, Ed Jones, and Dana Lynn Driscoll

Impetus for Research

In 2011, our research team developed the Writing Transfer Project, a multi-institutional, mixed-methods research study that investigated students' development and transfer-of-writing-related knowledge in first-year writing (FYW) and the following year. Administrators at our four universities had asked about the outcomes of writing instruction and its links to larger institutional concerns. In particular, they posed these questions: What knowledge and skills are students learning in FYW? What knowledge are they transferring—or not transferring—into subsequent courses, particularly courses in the disciplines? How effectively does our curriculum support students' writing development? Such questions are pressing, because, like many institutions, ours must demonstrate to accreditors the effective assessment of writing instruction.

Our results offer insight into specific types of writing knowledge that helped students transition successfully from high school to FYW and from FYW to writing in the disciplines. They also reveal potential barriers to the second transition. Our analysis foregrounds the role of genre awareness and metacognition in promoting transfer and shows how institutions can better support transfer from FYW to disciplinary courses.

Successful transfer of writing knowledge and skills is particularly challenging because the functions—and thus the features—of written genres differ significantly from one context to another. Although *adaptation* of originally learned skills in any subject area is needed to meet the demands of a new context, successful transfer of *writing* knowledge and skills faces the additional challenge of writers having to engage with new genres as they move into new disciplinary contexts. Such adaptations often require students to set aside previously learned conventions, textual features, or strategies to produce new genres with significantly different features (Nowacek, 2011; Reiff & Bawarshi, 2011; Wardle, 2007, 2009).

Genres are textual forms that develop in response to recurrent situations; they thus have typified formal features. These features enable writers to address the specific, recurring needs of users in particular contexts (Bawarshi & Reiff, 2010). For instance, academics use the related genres of calls for papers, conference proposals, conference papers, articles, and abstracts to publicize and seek feedback on their research. As students transition from FYW to disciplinary writing, they must write in new genres, for new audiences and purposes, adapting what they've learned previously about different genres and writing contexts. Writing transfer entails substantial complexity as students move across contexts and is thus unlikely to be smooth or perfect; the goal of our research is to enable students to make that transition as successfully as possible.

A National Research Council (2000) summary of research on transfer stressed that *cueing*, or graduated prompting designed to activate prior knowledge, is often needed to promote transfer of any skill or knowledge and advocated the use of scaled efforts to encourage retrieval and use of prior knowledge. Nowacek (2011), writing specifically about the transfer of writing skills, also emphasized the importance of cueing students' genre knowledge from earlier contexts to encourage transfer into new contexts. Nowacek contended, "Genre is not the only cue for transfer, but it is a powerful and underappreciated one" (p. 17). Cueing can take place within a course—a reminder to reflect on and assess whether to draw on skills learned in earlier assignments—or in later courses, as professors cue students to draw on and adapt prior knowledge or to recognize the need to incorporate new writing knowledge and skills. Recent studies have shown that many students fail to recognize the relevance of prior genre knowledge or to adapt it, whereas their more successful peers do repurpose such knowledge (Bergmann & Zepernick, 2007; Reiff & Bawarshi, 2011; Rounsaville, Goldberg, & Bawarshi, 2008).

To investigate transfer at these transitions, we studied student writing and students' perceptions of their writing longitudinally at four distinctly different institutions, examining student work both in FYW and in disciplinary writing. Our results show that the curricula studied successfully scaffold students' transition from high school to FYW but less effectively support the move from FYW to writing across the curriculum (WAC) or writing in the disciplines (WID). Furthermore, our results illustrate the principles that successful writing transfer involves repurposing prior knowledge and that institutions can promote such repurposing by teaching for transfer. Although our results refer to several types of writing knowledge, we interpret them through the lenses of work on genre and metacognition, which reveals how these types of writing knowledge intersect as students learn to produce academic genres that construct and disseminate disciplinary knowledge.

Contexts for Research Project and Research Methods

The Writing Transfer Project, a two-year study of student writing, used a data-rich, mixed-methods, multi-institutional, longitudinal design. We collected writing samples and student reflections on writing from undergraduate students at our four universities:

- A medium-sized northeastern, private, urban, Catholic, doctoral and research university
- A large mid-Atlantic, private, urban, research university (very high research activity)
- A large midwestern, public, urban, research university (very high research activity)
- A large midwestern, public, suburban, doctoral and research university

Our data included student work generated at each institution. Our results transcend local differences by comparing changes in students' paper scores across time (see www.understandingwritingtransfer.org for details).

Data Collection

We collected 58 paired sets of pre-FYW papers (P1), written prior to the study course (usually for a high school course), and end-of-FYW papers (P2), typically the last piece of source-based writing in the FYW course, from three participating universities (all but the large midwestern, public, urban university). We also collected 35 paired sets of end-of-FYW writing samples (P2) and year 2 writing samples (P3), collected during the first or second semester following the year 1 data collection, from all four universities. Finally, we also collected 398 reflections for 123 students in year 1 of the study; reflections were collected with each major writing project and in one or two early homework assignments in year 1. The reflections evaluated students' writing processes, discussed their learning, and described strengths and weaknesses.

Rating and Coding

We conducted two multiday analysis sessions in summers 2012 and 2013, with 24 and 31 graduate student coders, respectively. We trained coders using Lombard, Snyder-Duch, and Bracken's (2002) approach and maintained a minimum of 80% intercoder agreement. To rate writing samples, we developed a rubric that measured genre appropriateness so we could evaluate writing produced in high school, FYW, and disciplinary contexts. The rubric assessed how effectively texts met genre expectations, including use of sources, contextualization, and responsiveness to audience, purpose, and stylistic conventions. We stripped identifying features so raters did not know the papers' original contexts.

Key Findings Related to the Essential Principles

We explored two essential principles through the results of our research project: the need to adapt prior knowledge to new writing contexts (and what happens without such adaptations), and the need to "teach for transfer," particularly as students move from FYW to disciplinary writing.

Our study demonstrates that FYW effectively helps students make the transition from high school to college-level writing. Fifty-eight students, from three universities, submitted paired sets of pre-FYW and end-of-FYW writing samples; they showed a statistically significant *increase* in their total mean paper scores as they moved from high school to college writing, $t(57) = 3.65, p = .001$.

Moreover, genre awareness was significantly correlated with the increase in total mean scores from pre-FYW papers to end-of-FYW papers. Genre awareness links genre conventions with purpose and audience; it requires students to analyze new audience expectations and writing purposes to adapt prior knowledge to new writing contexts. Following Downs and Wardle (2007), we define *writing knowledge* as knowledge *about writing*; for instance, an explicit understanding of how genres function (versus writing skills, which are *composing strategies*, such as brainstorming, outlining, and evaluating a draft in light of assignment requirements). After we controlled for differences by university, genre awareness predicted the change from pre-FYW to end-of-FYW papers, $F(2, 55) = 5.56, p = .022$, adjusted $R^2 = .08$. That is, students who viewed genre as a means of inquiry and analysis, rather than as formulaic conventions, made the greatest gains in mean scores on the year 1 pre- to end-of-semester writing samples. Because these gains were statistically significant, this finding suggests both the efficacy of FYW in helping students transition from high school to college writing and the importance of genre awareness in their writing growth.

However, when students moved into new disciplinary writing contexts in year 2, writing sample scores declined at all four universities. For the 35 paired sets of end-of-FYW papers and year 2 papers, the change in the total mean scores showed a significant *decrease* when paired *t*-tests were run, $t(34) = -3.89, p < .001$. This decline suggests that students need extra support as they transition from FYW to disciplinary writing, although two of the four universities have WAC or WID programs. Furthermore, there was a lack of significant correlation between student reflections on genre from year 1 and the changes in writing sample scores from year 1 to year 2, implying that students did not successfully transfer genre awareness into the year 2 writing context.

Instead, we found that frequent reference to prior high school writing knowledge in students' year 1 reflections *predicted the decline* from year 1 to year 2 writing sample scores. Why might this correlation exist? Although writing instruction across U.S. high schools varies widely, students at our four institutions typically reported a high school emphasis on formulaic structures and approaches rather than on the need to adapt genres or other writing knowledge to new contexts (illustrating Adler-Kassner's [this volume] concerns with secondary standards). Students who in FYW reflected extensively on prior high school writing knowledge showed a dependence on this more rule-bound, high-school-based understanding of writing. Our findings suggest that FYW successfully helped students extend this understanding to adapt and repurpose writing strategies to new contexts, but when students left FYW for their year 2 disciplinary contexts, many students returned to the static, high-school-based approach. Such regression is not surprising, given that high schools typically provide students with four years of writing instruction, in five class periods per week, in contrast with one to two semesters of FYW instruction, meeting two or three times per week. An emphasis on formulaic approaches to writing may have left students unable to recognize—let alone fulfill—new disciplinary writing purposes and audience expectations. Thus, although FYW helps students transition from high school writing to college-level writing, its effects aren't strong enough alone to prepare students for the next critical transition: successful WID. Prior knowledge accounted for 11% of the declines in writing scores from semester 1 to semester 2, $\beta = -.46, t(30) = -3.21, p = .003$. (See Table 11.1 on the collection's website, www.understandingwritingtransfer.org)

Two factors did, however, seem to predict greater success in the year 2 writing task: use of sources and metacognition. Both of these concepts are related to what Michael Carter (2007) described as "metagenre." Metagenres—written forms used by groups of disciplines (Carter, 2007, pp. 393–394)—share features determined by disciplinary families' modes of inquiry and analysis, which construct disciplinary knowledge. For instance, Carter explained that the natural and social sciences, from psychology to physics, typically use empirical inquiry and related metagenres like the lab report, field note set, and IMRAD-structured research article (introduction, methods, results, analysis, and discussion). In contrast, research articles in humanities disciplines virtually never use IMRAD structures. Instead, humanities scholars construct arguments primarily from earlier texts (written, graphic, or cultural) and use related metagenres like the essay, critique, and purely theoretical article (published in these disciplines more often than in the sciences).

Although some textual features and argumentative moves are specific to particular metagenres, Carter (2007) noted that others cut across academic metagenres. The latter include the use of sources. In our study, student reflections on the use of sources predicted greater gains in student writing samples from the end of FYW to their disciplinary writing in year 2. Students who demonstrated this understanding of sources were developing facility with an important argumentative move in these metagenres, even though they may not have recognized the link between source use and genre. Helping them make such connections would encourage transfer by supporting their developing genre awareness. Source use accounted for 17% of the changes in students' writing scores from semester 1 to semester 2, $\beta = .36$, $t(30) = 2.53$, $p < .017$.

Second, we coded for metacognitive descriptions of how students applied and adapted their existing strategies and skills to a particular writing task; this code correlated with greater improvements in their texts, indicating a metacognitive awareness of the strategies used to produce particular genres and of how those strategies were adapted to produce new genres. This code's correlation with writing improvement from year 1 to year 2 suggests that conscious awareness of such adaptation helps students succeed in producing new genres and implies the importance of analyzing and adapting prior knowledge in this process. This code accounted for 10% of the changes made by students in writing scores from year 1 to year 2, $\beta = .44$, $t(30) = 2.50$, $p < .018$.

Carter (2007, p. 385) argued that his concept of metagenre could help disciplinary faculty understand genres as modes of inquiry and analysis, replacing the myth of writing as a static skill set with awareness that genres adapt across contexts to construct disciplinary knowledge. Such education for WAC and WID instructors is advocated by WAC and WID scholars (Carter, 2007; Condon & Rutz, 2012). Disciplinary faculty who can cue— and continue to develop—the writing knowledge students gain in FYW could help students revise formulaic, secondary-school views of writing by connecting their understanding of source use and other genre features to a metacognitive awareness of the strategies used to produce genres and of how genres construct disciplinary knowledge.

Preparing WAC and WID instructors to provide these cues requires an institution to develop a culture of effective writing instruction based on a campus-wide recognition that writing occurs not in an all-purpose form but in flexible genres with features determined by their purposes in particular disciplinary contexts. WAC and WID instructors can use such cues to encourage *transfer-focused thinking*, which we define as metacognitive awareness of writing strategies understood through genre and related concepts.

Implications for Curriculum Design and Faculty Development

Although our small sample size means that further research is needed to draw definitive conclusions about how to promote writing transfer from FYW to WAC and WID, our findings augment WAC and WID scholarship by offering the following steps, which institutions can take to promote such a campus culture:

- Institutions can support departments in designating and rewarding disciplinary writing faculty liaisons who take long-term responsibility for promoting effective disciplinary writing instruction by working closely with WAC and WID specialists.
- Institutions can support WAC and WID specialists in developing partnerships with disciplinary writing instructors. These partnerships must prepare disciplinary instructors to cue students to *reflect metacognitively* on the adaptations to prior writing strategies needed as students enter a new course by asking questions like the following:
  - What prior writing knowledge can be adapted, and what new knowledge must be learned to produce disciplinary writing?
    - For instance, what new genres are required for this new writing context? What audiences and purposes will the new genres serve?
    - What textual features and argumentative moves do these genres use? What features and moves do they share with genres familiar to students? What features and moves are new or different?
    - What role do sources play, and what strategies are needed to work effectively with them in disciplinary genres?

- Institutions can encourage writing programs to collect assessment data on students' developing genre and metacognitive awareness, as well as on other aspects of writing knowledge and skill, and to use it to improve curricula, teaching strategies, and connections between FYW and WAC and WID instruction. Broad research is still necessary; for instance, a larger sample size might make visible additional factors that could enable students to make more successful transitions to disciplinary writing contexts.

Such efforts are likely to require trust building across groups (opening opportunities for knotworking; see Werder, this volume). For instance, seeing that students who have passed FYW often still do not write as well as hoped, disciplinary faculty sometimes suspect that FYW programs are ineffective. FYW programs and university administrators must clearly communicate the challenges students face in moving into new writing contexts and the fact that college- and professional-level writing expertise typically develops over several years. Furthermore, administrators must incentivize WAC and WID instructors' participation in professional development, assessment initiatives, and cross-disciplinary coordination, which demand substantial time and energy. Such incentives must engage all WAC and WID instructors, from full-time faculty, to part-time faculty, to graduate students. By grounding such efforts in assessment findings on students' genre awareness and other writing knowledge, institutions can show accreditors and others how they use a data-driven approach to improve writing instruction.

References

Bawarshi, A. S., & Reiff, M. J. (2010). *Genre: An introduction to history, theory, research, and pedagogy.* West Lafayette, IN: Parlor.

Bergmann, L. S., & Zepernick, J. (2007). Disciplinarity and transfer: Students' perceptions of learning to write. *WPA: Writing Program Administration, 31*(1–2), 124–149.

Carter, M. (2007). Ways of knowing, doing, and writing in the disciplines. *College Composition and Communication, 58*(3), 385–418.

Condon, W., & Rutz, C. (2012, December). A taxonomy of writing across the curriculum programs: Evolving to serve broader agendas. *College Composition and Communication, 64*(2), 357–382.

Downs, D., & Wardle, E. (2007, June). Teaching about writing, righting misconceptions: (Re)envisioning "first-year composition" as "introduction to writing studies." *College Composition and Communication, 58*(4), 552–584.

Lombard, M., Snyder-Duch, J., & Bracken, C. C. (2002). Content analysis in mass communication: Assessment and reporting of intercoder reliability. *Human Communication Research, 28*(4), 587–604.

National Research Council. (2000). *How people learn: Brain, mind, experience, and school.* Washington, DC: National Academy Press.

Nowacek, R. (2011). *Agents of integration: Understanding transfer as a rhetorical act.* Carbondale, IL: Southern Illinois University Press.

Reiff, M. J., & Bawarshi, A. (2011). Tracing discursive resources: How students use prior genre knowledge to negotiate new writing contexts in first-year composition. *Written Communication, 28*(3), 312–337.

Rounsaville, A., Goldberg, R., & Bawarshi, A. (2008). From incomes to outcomes: FYW students' prior genre knowledge, metacognition, and the question of transfer. *WPA: Writing Program Administration, 32*(1–2), 97–112.

Wardle, E. (2007). Understanding "transfer" from FYC: Preliminary results of a longitudinal study. *WPA: Writing Program Administration, 31*(1–2), 65–85.

Wardle, E. (2009). "Mutt genres" and the goal of FYC: Can we help students write the genres of the university? *College Composition and Communication, 60*(4), 765–789.

12

PROMOTING CROSS-DISCIPLINARY TRANSFER

A Case Study in Genre Learning

Mary Goldschmidt

Impetus for Research

As this volume shows, writing transfer from first-year composition to other contexts is a complex process dependent on a number of factors. The difficulty students have in seeing similarities between what they learn in their first-year writing courses and what they encounter elsewhere in the curriculum is compounded in the transition from the humanities to the sciences, where the differences seem especially pronounced. What insights for programmatic and curricular design can we learn from examining these critical transitions?

Beginning in 2005, I had the opportunity to help implement a writing in the disciplines (WID) curriculum, providing support for departments as they identified and redesigned their designated writing-intensive (WI) courses. Two majors in particular, psychology and computer science, developed sophomore-level courses that focused on early exposure to the scientific research article as intentional preparation for senior-level research writing in the capstone course. These departments thus provided an opportunity to examine writing development through mastery of genre when students cross disciplinary boundaries in the movement from general education requirements into their major.

The field of rhetorical genre studies provides the most useful lens for understanding the challenges faced in this consequential transition. We know, for example, that humanities-based first-year composition courses and technical communication courses can't actually teach the genres that students will later encounter in their disciplinary course work, because the students are not yet doing the disciplinary activities that provide the exigency for the genre (Artemeva, 2008; Brent, 2011; Ford, 2004; Freedman, 1994; Russell & Yanez, 2003; Wardle, 2009). As Wardle (2009) discovered, even when writing courses are linked with a disciplinary course in the students' major (e.g., biology), genre learning is difficult, impeded largely by the students' lack of experience in doing the work of that discipline and the consequent lack of understanding of the role of the genre in that system: "The students were not working in biology, thus they (and she) were not able to understand or even mimic the genres that mediate work in the biology activity system" (p. 780).

An additional problem is that even in technical communication courses designed to prepare students specifically for the writing required in the sciences, students tend only to be able to transfer stylistic or formatting knowledge. For example, Ford's (2004) study of transfer from a technical communication course to an industrial engineering course reveals that rather than relying on "awareness of audience or sense of purpose" to guide their writing decisions, students instead focused on "model-based tactics, formats and templates, and the text's appearance" (p. 310). In other words, they still see genre as a form, not as an action within a rhetorical context. As a result, Ford recommended in her "Implications for the Classroom" section that faculty members not teach genres as *products* or "as templates into which they can just plug the right words" (p. 311). Instead, she suggested that we teach what genres *are* and not what they look like, a move that is similar to the "Writing About Writing" curricula developed by Downs and Wardle (2007).

Ford (2004) found that students were, however, able to transfer rhetorical awareness from workplace writing experiences such as co-ops and internships, and thus she concluded, "In order for students to fully grasp rhetorical strategies that call for conceptual thinking and problem solving, they need to have experience writing texts in a context besides the classroom. Within this [classroom] context, the audiences they write for are not staged, and thus, seem more real" (p. 310). The realness Ford invoked here supports conclusions from activity theory that insist on immersion models as the only effective way to teach genre. Brent (2011), for example, following Freedman (1994), contended that learning a new genre requires situated learning contexts: "Highly context-dependent skills such as rhetorical performance are best learned—perhaps can only be learned—when learners are immersed in the real context in which such skills must be performed on a daily basis" (p. 400). Exposure over time and within a community of practice is thus crucial for genre learning.

For *academic* genres, however, the community of practice is, in fact, the classroom and interaction with professors, insofar as the "real" context for these genres is the academy. Thus, the question remains: How can we create curricular experiences that teach for transfer when the dissimilarities among genres in the humanities and the sciences discourage transfer?

Context for Research Project and Research Methods

This study was conducted at a midsize, four-year state college in the mid-Atlantic region of the United States, where each major at the college requires three WI courses: a first-year seminar in any discipline, a mid-level WI course in the sophomore or junior year, and a WI capstone course in the senior year. For psychology majors, the mid-level WI course is a research seminar involving a full empirical study conducted by students in small groups; they spend the entire semester writing all four sections (introduction, methods, results, and discussion) using American Psychological Association (APA) format. In the comparable mid-level WI course for computer science majors (on software engineering), students write papers in which they justify software application recommendations; here, the faculty member provides a template that uses many of the conventions of Association for Computing Machinery papers, even though students are not conducting research.

Over the course of the 2012 spring semester, I conducted 10 in-depth, text-based interviews with two groups of students: seniors whose records indicated that they had mastered their discipline's primary research genre, and sophomores who were in the early stages of learning those genres. Interview questions included open-ended inquiries about students' development as writers over the course of their college career (including experiences that fostered that development), as well as text-based questions in which they were prompted to discuss specific passages. I was most interested in learning which activities students perceived to have been most helpful as they negotiated this lengthy consequential transition, and I used constructivist grounded theory (Charmaz, 2002, 2006) to analyze the transcripts.

Key Findings Related to the Essential Principles

This analysis highlights several challenges students face as they navigate transitions into disciplinary writing. Yet, the interview findings also suggest factors that can promote transfer of learning across disciplinary contexts.

Two Critical Transition Points: First Encounters With Science Writing and Learning the Scientific Research Article Genre

Students who major in the sciences often face stark differences in both the stylistic and structural expectations for writing compared to what is routinely (and often unquestioningly) expected in humanities-based general education courses (Berkenkotter, 2000; Giltrow, 2000). The new modes are unfamiliar enough to require high-road transfer, and yet students don't often make the mindful abstractions necessary for repurposing what might be relevant from previous contexts. For example, participants saw categorical differences between humanities-based writing ("flowery," "prosey," "verbose," and "expressive") and scientific writing ("analytical" or "making statements and facts"). Sophomore psychology major Nicole said it best: "In high school and probably like my first semester here, I was always really good at English kind of writing and analytical kind of writing in that way. And then with psych as my major I really had to learn a whole new kind of writing, a scientific kind of writing."

There were also references to deeper, epistemological differences. Like the students in Bergmann and Zepernick's study (2007) who saw "English" writing as an invitation to "share their own convictions, opinions, and experiences in a way that is primarily expressive, subjective and creative" (p. 130), my participants talked about how they were "used to kind of just being able to conjecture and say what I'm thinking" and how now "you can't just say something, you have to back it up."

These differences in style and the seemingly new ways of supporting claims were made more difficult to negotiate, in part, because they are being encountered in the context of what seem like alien structures. As psychology senior Michelle explained,

> The first time I encountered writing like this was in 121 [a prerequisite to the WI course], where even then I was like, "What's a methods section, why would you put that into a formal paper?" It seems more of something that would be an appendix, or just like something separate, because it breaks the flow of the paper, cause, I thought, because it was another title, why would you, you know? That was the first time I ever encountered having to write like that and at first it was very bizarre. Now when I look at every other class, I think, "Why aren't they like psych papers, it would make so much more sense."

As a senior, she internalized the logic of the genre, but early on the differences were befuddling.

Nearly all of the participants referred to the helpfulness of the templates provided by their professors when they were first learning the scientific research article. Psychology sophomore Nicole referred explicitly to looking at the template for guidance when writing the introduction: "Put an idea here and then give me some articles that support it. And put your next idea here and give me some articles that support it. And then after all that tell me how that leads up to what you're going to do." Although the first level of performance with a template is rhetorically unaware, it often provides the building blocks for later, more self-reflective composition.

The descriptions of writing the scientific research article provided by senior participants indicate that they have internalized the norms of science writing and have been able to repurpose their sense of authorship for this new community. How they grappled with the challenges of the introduction, in particular—with its "unnerving wealth of options" as a complex rhetorical construct (Swales, 1990, p. 137)—illustrates a growing sense of rhetorical agency and disciplinary membership. Cecelia's work with a mediational hypothesis and multiple causal variables, for example, required that she take "something that was largely psycho-linguistic and make it into like a clinical construct." At this point, it is self-identification as a practitioner in the field—not the template—that enables her proficiency in science writing. In Danny's account of writing his introduction, too, we can see that he is no longer following a template but trying to meet the needs of his readers. He understands that it must contextualize and justify the questions at the heart of his study in a way that leads the reader to see the gap, absence, or contradiction being addressed: "You have to find things that, things in existing research that are not talked about enough, not talked about at all, that are confusing or contradictory."

Factors That Promote Cross-Disciplinary Transfer

As we have seen, the complexity of writing transfer is compounded when students face the seemingly alien terrain of the sciences after years of writing instruction in both secondary school and early college curricula that are dominated by implicit humanities-based writing norms. However, the factors that correlate with the self-conscious awareness of disciplinary writing so central for advanced genre learning are (a) an extensive exposure to different disciplinary standards through double majors or minors and (b) involvement in what Prior (1998) called the "deep participation" of disciplinary enculturation, namely, "strong and growing access to disciplinary discourses, practices, and relationships" (p. 133).

Although most senior participants were able to see differences among the genres in their various courses as *disciplinary* differences, and not simply as the "idiosyncratic" differences of individual professors (Thaiss & Zawacki, 2006, p. 139), those who had double majors or minors or who had switched majors had more nuanced understandings of subdisciplinary variations and of interdisciplinary differences. Such an awareness is essential for the conscious strategizing needed for writing in an unfamiliar context. Danny, for example, who was originally a biology major but changed to a major in psychology and a minor in statistics, could easily locate his own subfield within the larger psychology domain, and he could also perceive how a faculty member's area of specialization would shape the writing expectations in each class in the various sections of the mid-level WI course: In "one section that professor could be an industrial organizational psychologist, but then another professor teaching a different section could be a clinical psychologist." As a result, he realized that there is no universal way to write in psychology; compositional choices are rhetorically based and thus more transferable.

Michelle, a psychology major with a minor in marketing, could explicitly talk about similarities and differences across disciplinary fields. She was able to use her understanding of the research genre in psychology to complete the required paper in a 300-level marketing course, a transfer success that not all her peers achieved: "I could tell a lot of the [business] students were confused as to why it was like almost like a science paper and not a theoretical essay."

The higher level of interdisciplinary awareness acquired by students with more disciplinary exposure also points to their recognition of the need for rhetorical instruction and direct experience doing the work of the discipline. Danny was able to identify the cause of his difficulty in a 300-level general education history course precisely as his lack of membership in that activity system: "I've never been more in the dark in a class than I was in that class. I had never taken a history course in college. I was not a history major. I had never been introduced to history writing: what should be there, what shouldn't be there, what was important, what wasn't."

Exposure to other disciplines, however, isn't always enough to foster the kind of awareness of disciplinary differences necessary for cross-disciplinary writing success. Justin's experience as a double major in computer science and economics illustrates the need for experiences beyond taking required classes, because his understanding of the research article in computer science did not translate into easy application or integration in his other field of study. Also essential are things like presenting at conferences and being involved in professors' research projects—both of which depend on developing relationships with faculty. Justin cited the lack of this kind of "access to disciplinary discourses, practices, and relationships" (Prior, 1998, p. 133) as the main reason he still had "no idea what to do" in his economics thesis. Justin also noted his deeper relationships with professors from the computer science department, who he feels have "cared for, nurtured me more than the other."

Justin's sense of these relationships signals the centrality of identity in the transfer process: Consequential transitions are successfully negotiated when the individual can see himself or herself as a member of the new community of practice. All but one of the senior participants described the importance of weekly meetings with thesis advisers and the presence of mentors, experience in submitting proposals for conferences, intentions to publish and awareness of peers who have been published, and participation in joint faculty–student research projects.

Implications for Curriculum Design

My case study findings illustrate that cross-disciplinary transfer involves a conscious and consequential transformation of participants' identities as contributing members of an academic discourse community. However, the fact that disciplinary genre learning and a sense of identity as a discourse community member are mutually constitutive over time (Bawarshi, 2003; Bazerman, 2009; Prior, 1998) tends to work against easy cross-disciplinary transfer when students have only one experience of disciplinary encultura-tion and when such transfer is expected to take place quickly. Transforming prior genre knowledge for such a significantly new context as the sciences is a lengthy process, one that points to curricular changes at the institutional level and the programmatic level.

Successful cross-disciplinary transfer will require, for example, more robust genre learning in general education courses such that students experience writing as explicitly situated in a community of practice. My case study provides additional support for Brent's (2011) contention that "any rhetorical knowledge that we want to stick will need to be woven through the fabric of rhetorical education" (p. 411). Examples include new first-year writing models, already underway in composition studies, in which students are not taught humanities genres as universal academic genres but instead introduced to the concept of genre as a construct that they can observe and analyze in a variety of contexts (see also Robertson & Taczak, this volume).

In addition, institutions may want to consider initiatives that jump start the teaching of genre in all disciplinary contexts so that when students move from one context to another, they bring a metagenre awareness and can look for how a specific genre works within its community of practice: what exigencies evoke its production, how its structure fulfills its purpose and therefore meets readers' expectations, and so on. Miami University's West-ern Program (previously known as the School of Interdisciplinary Studies from 1974–2008) provides a replicable four-year model in which attention to eventual cross-disciplinary transfer is made a priority as early as stage one (Haynes, 1996).

Expanding the scope of rhetorical instruction also points to greater investment in living and learning communities, service-learning courses, and problem-based learning where rhetorically focused writing is a central part of these experiences. Ultimately, all of these fronts point to a very different model of general education, not one that is menu and "breadth" exposure based but instead one that is extended interdisciplinary sequences using problem-based learning or other high-impact experiences as advanced by Kuh (2008). Feldman (2008) outlined one such approach in *Making Writing*

Matter and advocated contextualizing writing within collaborative scholarship between faculty and local community organizations.

More needs to be done and can be done across the curriculum to give students—however briefly—a sense of writing as *action within a community*. Higher education leaders will need to explore how we can best foster enhanced rhetorical awareness, increase our students' exposure to how and why the members of a disciplinary discourse community share their research, and expand experiences that generate the motivation of communicating one's own research. Providing students with firsthand exposure to how the writing in a discipline is a social action will help them become more fully empowered writers in any context.

References

Artemeva, N. (2008). Toward a unified theory of genre learning. *Journal of Business and Technical Communication, 22*, 160–185.

Bawarshi, A. (2003). *Genre and the invention of the writer*. Logan, UT: Utah State University Press.

Bazerman, C. (2009). Genre and cognitive development: Beyond writing to learn. In C. Bazerman, A. Bonini, & D. Figueiredo (Eds.), *Genre in a changing world* (pp. 279–294). Fort Collins, CO: WAC Clearinghouse and Parlor Press. Retrieved from http://wac.colostate.edu/books/genre

Bergmann, L., & Zepernick, J. (2007). Disciplinarity and transference: Students' perceptions of learning to write. *WPA: Writing Program Administration, 31*(1–2), 124–149.

Berkenkotter, C. (2000). Scientific writing and scientific thinking: Writing the scientific habit of mind. In M. Goggin (Ed.), *Inventing a discipline: Rhetoric scholarship in honor of Richard E. Young* (pp. 270–284). Urbana, IL: NCTE.

Brent, D. (2011). Transfer, transformation, and rhetorical knowledge: Insights from transfer theory. *Journal of Business and Technical Communication, 25*, 396–420.

Charmaz, K. (2002). Qualitative interviewing and grounded theory analysis. In J. Gubrium & J. Holstein (Eds.), *Handbook of interview research: Context and method* (pp. 675–694). London, UK: Sage.

Charmaz, K. (2006). *Constructing grounded theory: A practical guide through qualitative analysis*. Thousand Oaks, CA: Sage.

Downs, D., & Wardle, E. (2007). Teaching about writing, righting misconceptions: (Re)envisioning "first-year composition" as "introduction to writing studies." *College Composition and Communication, 58*(4), 552–584.

Feldman, A. (2008). *Making writing matter: Composition in the engaged university*. Albany, NY: SUNY Press.

Ford, J. D. (2004). Knowledge transfer across the disciplines: Tracking rhetorical strategies from a technical communication classroom to an engineering classroom. *IEE Transactions on Professional Communication, 47*(4), 301–315.

Freedman, A. (1994). "Do as I say": The relationship between teaching and learning new genres. In A. Freedman & P. Medway (Eds.), *Genre and the new rhetoric* (pp. 191–210). London, UK: Taylor and Francis.

Giltrow, J. (2000). "Argument" as a term in talk about student writing. In S. Mitchell & R. Andrews (Eds.), *Learning to argue in higher education* (pp. 129–145). Portsmouth, NH: Boynton/Cook.

Haynes, C. (1996). Interdisciplinary writing and the undergraduate experience: A four-year writing plan proposal. *Issues in Integrative Studies, 14*, 29–57.

Kuh, G. (2008). *High-impact educational practices: What they are, who has access to them and why they matter.* Washington, DC: Association of American Colleges & Universities.

Prior, P. (1998). *Writing/disciplinarity: A sociohistoric account of literate activity in the academy.* Mahwah, NJ: Lawrence Erlbaum.

Russell, D., & Yanez, A. (2003). "Big picture people rarely become historians": Genre systems and the contradictions of general education. In C. Bazerman & D. Russell (Eds.), *Writing selves/writing societies* (pp. 331–362). Fort Collins, CO: WAC Clearinghouse and Mind, Culture, and Activity. Retrieved from http://wac.colostate.edu/books/selves_societies

Swales, J. (1990). *Genre analysis: English in academic and research settings.* Cambridge, UK: Cambridge University Press.

Thaiss, C., & Zawacki, T. M. (2006). *Engaged writers and dynamic disciplines: Research on the academic writing life.* Portsmouth, NH: Boynton/Cook.

Wardle, E. (2009). "Mutt genres" and the goal of FYC: Can we help students write the genres of the university? *College Composition and Communication, 60*(4), 765–789.

13

"THE HARDEST THING WITH WRITING IS NOT GETTING ENOUGH INSTRUCTION"

Helping Educators Guide Students Through Writing Challenges

Elizabeth Wardle and Nicolette Mercer Clement

Impetus for Research

Educators hope and expect that as students move through their educational experiences, they will be able to build on their prior knowledge to complete new tasks and learn new material. This hope is what we might call the "hope for transfer." Yet, designing educational experiences that facilitate learning in this way is difficult, as many researchers have pointed out. Perkins and Salomon (1992) noted that education can achieve abundant transfer if designed to do so but that most educational experiences are not designed to do so. Frustrations with what teachers see as lack of transfer are especially apparent when it comes to writing. Teachers and professionals at all levels have remained frustrated with student writing for over a century and a half—since writing in English became a usual part of the American educational curriculum (see Russell, 2002).

Yet, the good news is that we do not have to remain frustrated. Research about transfer and writing transfer in particular has increasingly provided information that can, with some careful planning and support from stakeholders, improve student writing and better enable students to draw on what they already know about writing and know how to do with writing to engage new and increasingly difficult writing tasks.

In this chapter, we will discuss research findings that illustrate some of the challenges that students face as they write across their college courses. We will consider some of the factors that make writing tasks challenging for students, what constrains them from drawing on prior knowledge and effectively using it to engage those challenges, and what affordances assist students (or could better assist students) in this work.

Context for Research Project and Research Methods

As the introduction to this collection noted, *transfer* is not a simple ability to carry and reuse a skill or piece of information. Although easy and unconscious reuse of prior knowledge can happen in near transfer, far transfer is a much more complex phenomenon. Many if not most new writing challenges during college cannot be considered near transfer, even though faculty members often assume that students will experience them as such. Instead, students find that to complete a new and challenging writing task, they must not only draw on what they know but also repurpose or generalize it so that it works effectively for the task at hand; in addition, such writing challenges also tend to involve learning something new in the process. A number of writing scholars have drawn on activity theorist Yrgö Engeström's (1987) work to call this type of transfer "creative repurposing for expansive learning" (Prior & Shipka, 2003; Roozen, 2010). These sorts of cognitive challenges tend to happen in the space that cognitive psychologist Lev Vygotsky (1978) called the "zone of proximal development," wherein a learner cannot perform the new task alone but could perform the new task with appropriate types of support or what sociocultural theorists call "scaffolding" (Obukhova & Korepanova, 2009).

What enables people to act effectively within a zone of proximal development? Many things do, including the ability to see what they already know as relevant and the ability to know how to use it for the current task that is beyond what they know. In addition, the environment (including the educational setting and its teachers, tools, and dispositions) must provide appropriate affordances (supports) for action that are perceived as affordances by the learner. Affordances provide writers the possibility of acting in a particular environment. However, affordance lies not in the object or in the person but in the relationship between them (Bærentsen & Trettvik, 2002). As Engeström noted in a famous example (Bærentsen & Trettvik, 2002), for a person to sit on a chair, she must perceive the chair as sit-on-able. If she does not, the chair does not provide an affordance for resting. Or, she may not need to rest, in which case the chair is not an affordance for what she does need.

To illustrate the constraints and affordances of writing—and transferring writing skills and knowledge—across college classrooms, we will draw on an ongoing longitudinal case study of Nicolette Mercer Clement, a nursing student at the University of Central Florida and coauthor of this chapter. Nicolette was a student in a first-year composition course taught by Elizabeth Wardle (also a coauthor of this chapter) and was recruited by Wardle to participate in a study documenting all the writing-related challenges she faced throughout her time in college. Rather than studying Nicolette without sharing the purpose of the study, Wardle invited her to be a coresearcher, because only she could identify where her struggles lay. She agreed to contact Wardle (via text message) each time she encountered writing challenges, share all the texts she wrote for her course work (via Evernote), and then meet with Wardle to discuss how she approached the challenges she faced; several times she determined that she should record herself throughout the composing process for a particular text to look more closely at how she engaged challenges. The two of us have spent a great deal of time looking at the resources and situations that enabled Nicolette to effectively draw on prior knowledge to learn how to complete new writing tasks in new situations, as well as the ways in which she was constrained from doing so. Here we will draw on the data that we have collected to tell a story that illustrates some of the struggles students face when writing in college, as well as the framing, support, resources, and skills that can enable them to successfully take on these challenges. From Nicolette's experiences, we will suggest some principles that can guide teachers and administrators as they design programs, courses, and assignments.

Key Findings Related to the Essential Principles

Perkins and Salomon (1992) said that most school tasks are not designed to teach for transfer but that "education can achieve abundant transfer if designed to do so," a point also emphasized in Principle 4 (university programs can "teach for transfer"). Nicolette's experiences bear out their claims. In general education courses, she struggled to bring to bear what she knew to complete new tasks with little or confusing support. But her experiences, especially in her nursing classes, also make clear that education *can* be designed to teach for transfer and to enable students to draw on what they know and use the affordances in the situation to learn about new ideas and write in new ways. However, many programs and courses are not currently designed in this way, and many faculty members and administrators carry misconceptions about writing that keep them from redesigning courses and assignments to better facilitate student learning. A common fear of plagiarism—or, less dramatically, a fear that examples discourage creativity—often keeps faculty members from providing sample texts for students. Teachers also often fear that if students share ideas, they might not do their own work. Teachers also have a tendency to see "errors" in student writing and attribute them to laziness or lack of editing when, in fact, students' struggles with new content and conventions may be making it difficult for them to produce polished texts. All of these common fears and misconceptions are detrimental to student learning. Learners need examples, they need to work through new and challenging ideas with others, and they need time to explore new ideas through less polished writing before being expected to produce more polished writing. If teachers and administrators can change their thinking about how writing and learning happen, we can all do a better job of helping students repurpose for expansive learning in their zones of proximal development.

In sum, the data from this longitudinal study suggest three key findings that are clearly related to the essential principles outlined in the introduction to this collection. We will summarize the key findings here and then discuss them (and their implications) more fully after describing the data. These findings clearly illustrate Principle 2, which states that writing transfer is an extremely complex phenomenon.

First, students need to be taught specific rhetorical strategies that assist them in analyzing new texts so that they can successfully approach and compose those texts (this finding emphasizes Principle 4, that particular kinds of instruction can inform transfer).

Second, even well-honed analysis skills are not sufficient when students are unfamiliar with course content and conventions of new disciplines or professions. Students require time to become familiar with content and community conventions before their analysis and composing skills can enable them to effectively write in new and extremely different situations.

Third, students need teacher feedback when tackling new writing tasks, but rigid rules focused on format and correctness can actually impede learning.

Nicolette's Case: Navigating Affordances and Constraints in Challenging School Writing Tasks

In what follows, we will consider particular writing-related challenges that Nicolette encountered that required her to engage in active repurposing of prior knowledge to learn something new and complete the task at hand. These are the sorts of challenges that make teaching difficult, but helping students through them is the task of educators. We will examine the affordances and constraints that affected Nicolette's abilities to move effectively through her zones of proximal development.

What Makes School Writing Tasks Challenging?

During her first five semesters at UCF, Nicolette compiled a fairly long list of tasks she felt to be challenging. These included a reflective journal, a cover letter and application, weekly "one-minute essays," take-home midterm essays, a website review, essays on art and sexuality, and nursing care plans.

These tasks varied in level of challenge, and Nicolette experienced them as challenging for different reasons. For example, the cover letter was challenging because she had never written one before, and the reflective journal was challenging because she was gaining intellectual curiosity about the ideas she was being exposed to. She appeared to have and use effective strategies in responding to these challenges, drawing on prior knowledge and skills not only about the genre but also about how the genres work and how to reflect on and analyze genres. For the cover letter, for example, she collected examples, looked at their similarities and differences, figured out where there was wiggle room, and then drafted and revised. In an interview, Nicolette described how she went about writing a cover letter for the first time. She located cover letter directions through an Internet search but determined that she really needed to look at examples so that she could see where the examples varied:

> I read through the example and then I looked at the template and *compared if it fit exactly, if there was a little lenience that could be a little different.* And then, based on that and based on things that I thought would be good for the experience that I've had and for this . . . position, *[I] changed things a little bit, but mostly it still fit the same format because so did the example that I got from a completely different website.* [It] still fit this basic template. So I figured it needs to be somewhat strict like that.

She recognized that there was no single format or magic formula for all cover letters, but her careful analysis of examples helped her to see what was expected and where in her words, "there would be a little wiggle room."

To be able to engage in the new task, Nicolette drew on her previous knowledge about what genres are and how they work (e.g., that there are similarities across them but also individual difference), as well as her knowledge that examples are useful and her ability to find and usefully analyze examples by looking for similarities and differences across them. Furthermore, Nicolette was able to use what she learned from this analysis to write her own cover letter.

Although her analysis and reflection abilities were strong, Nicolette encountered challenges wherein those abilities were not enough. At times, for example, she did not know enough about the material to write in a way that would stand up to an expert's reading; she needed to elaborate on ideas but was not sure how to do so, and she did not understand the written conventions, lexis (specialized language), or insider expectations of a particular discipline. She employed a variety of strategies when responding to such challenges, including analyzing what might be required, imagining audience expectations, drafting and planning in advance, explicitly considering previous tasks that might assist her with the current task, soliciting feedback from others, and attempting to understand and respond to teacher feedback. Such strategies enabled her to act and complete challenging tasks in Western Civilization and Honors Seminar, but they did not enable her to complete the tasks with the level of competence both she and her teachers wanted.

She needed additional resources, information, and support from her instructors to move to that level of competence. At times these resources and support were simply not available; at other times, the resources and support the teachers attempted to provide had negative consequences (unintended but still very real).

For example, although Nicolette knew to analyze what new texts should look like, in Western Civilization and Honors Seminar, she was not given sample texts that she could analyze, and she could not easily find such examples on her own, as she had done with the cover letter. In addition, the instructions and expectations were often unclear. The Western Civilization midterm directions (see Figure 13.1) included only the test questions and then information for how to submit to turnitin (i.e., a tool that estimates that original content in student drafts against a database of published and student papers, checking for plagiarism), which included a word requirement, the admonition to fasten the turnitin receipt to the front of the paper, and a warning about letter grade deductions for each "infraction."

Figure 13.1. Western Civilization teacher's e-mailed directions.

1. You must upload BOTH your answers on the same site.
2. Print out the receipt and fasten (paper clip or staple only) it to the front of the paper you turn in to me.
3. The copy that you turn in at class should be double spaced in Times New Roman 14 point font.
4. The question you are answering must be at the beginning of each essay.
5. The length of your paper should be between 500 and 800 words.
6. Failure to fulfill any of these guidelines will result in a grade letter deduction for each infraction.

Clearly, the teacher was attempting to provide explicit instructions, but the instructions were all about procedures—stapling, font size, and word count. These instructions did not provide the guidance that Nicolette needed about the kinds of information that should be included or about the appropriate conventions for talking about that information (e.g., level of formality, types of citations that should be used, etc.).

As a result of the lack of examples and explicit content- and convention-related instruction, she often found herself guessing about what the conventions should be: In the case of the Western Civilization midterm, she made guesses about, for example, whether to explicitly cite her sources (she decided she should not) and whether to use "I" (again, she decided she should not). When we discussed how she came to the conclusion that she shouldn't use "I," she said, "I don't know, except it just seemed we weren't supposed to. Because a lot of times teachers preach not to put 'I' and stuff in your essays, and I figured he would probably be one of those teachers. And it just seemed like a paper where you wouldn't be putting your own—you wouldn't be saying it's your own thoughts. But I'm not really sure how I came to that conclusion."

New tasks were challenging to Nicolette not only because of unclear conventions and expectations but also because the content of her general education courses was often new to her. Nicolette's experiences illustrate that basic genre knowledge (e.g., knowledge of "the essay," which she wrote in both Western Civilization and Honors Seminar) was insufficient not only because the problem wasn't simply a lack of knowledge about what the individual instructor expected an essay to be like but also because of her lack of knowledge about what an essay about *those topics* (e.g., history and art) should be like, her lack of knowledge about those topics in general, and her inexperience with how disciplinary specialists talk about those topics. For example, her problems writing the Honors Seminar paper included not knowing much about art or philosophy and not knowing how the philosophy and literature professors coteaching the class expected her to use language in an essay. The first unit's paper in Honors Seminar, on what she described to me as "art and avant-garde versus kitsch," required her to write about terms she'd never heard before enrolling in that class. She explained that art was not something she had any prior experience with, though other students in the class did have such experience.

Noting how lack of content knowledge affects students' abilities to write in new settings is important, because faculty in all disciplines tend to talk about what students can transfer about writing as being somehow disconnected from content or situation. In other words, we tend to think about writing transfer solely in terms of skills. Yet, in Nicolette's writing, the phrasing and claims and even the punctuation suffer not because she can't write well in these ways but because she is not yet familiar enough with the content to form coherent statements. For example, Nicolette began the first draft of the first paper like this:

> There is no question that within every culture, there are representations of good art and bad art. How we define good versus bad art, however, always quickly proves to be a challenge.

Next to this the teacher wrote "EM," which according to the detailed key code she provided meant "empty phrase." The teacher was commenting on what she took to be a sentence-level problem, that Nicolette is using a phrase that doesn't mean anything. However, the reason that Nicolette wrote what she did was that she did not understand the material very well and had never talked about art before enrolling in this course just a few weeks prior to writing these opening sentences. The rest of her paper demonstrated the same problems repeatedly; in it, she used words and phrases that the teacher responded to by writing "RQ" (rhetorical question) or "What do you mean by this?" Of course, the reason Nicolette asked questions or wrote unclearly was that she was struggling to understand the material; she found it easier to write a question than make a statement, and she tried to use the phrases from the class reading without really understanding what those phrases meant.

Nicolette's experiences make clear that content, genre conventions, and lexis are all inextricably related and tied deeply to the social context. Her lack of content knowledge constrained her ability to bring her other prior knowledge to bear on a challenging task.

Affordances in the Zone of Proximal Development: Teacher Feedback and Peer Support

Teacher feedback plays an important role in growth when students bring some prior knowledge to bear but need assistance in learning disciplinary content and how disciplinary experts talk about that content. The feedback that Nicolette received on assignments across her courses varied widely, and its helpfulness varied as well. For example, on her Western Civilization midterms, the sole teacher response consisted of one question mark. The written response to her first Honors Seminar paper, on the other hand, was quite lengthy, consisting of a two-page corrections symbols handout that explained the many teacher marks on Nicolette's papers (e.g., EM = empty phrase), and a three-paragraph typed response stapled to the front, which noted "Improving the economy of prose will increase the clarity of your argument" and recommended that she "eliminate vague sentences" and attend to "writing mistakes." Nicolette was appreciative when she received the correction key in Honors Seminar, even though that key did not help her understand *why* a particular phrase might be marked as an EM. At least here she was receiving some information, not being forced to interpret one cryptic question mark.

Nonetheless, both kinds of responses—one almost nonexistent and one deeply detailed but focusing on correctness without explanation—had the effect of encouraging Nicolette to try hard to follow directions and figure out "what the teacher wanted," however vague or specific those expectations might have been, redirecting her focus from ideas and analysis to *correctness*, however the teacher defined that, and whether she understood the teacher's corrections. In many ways, these responses worked against Nicolette's learning; she carefully revised the Honors Seminar papers and received higher grades each time, but when she explained her revisions to me, she said that she corrected each item the teacher marked whether she understood it or not. She corrected rather than attempted to learn more about the ideas that her errors marked her as not yet understanding. The teacher provided no real incentive for further learning but a lot of incentive for following directions without understanding why she was making the corrections she was being asked to make.

Nicolette's experiences suggest that rhetorical tasks in school settings are often not effectively designed to encourage learning and mastery of new ideas and skills but instead (regardless of individual intention of the teacher) have the effect of encouraging students to figure out how to avoid error and obey rules that are rarely disclosed.

Yet, not all courses or teachers failed in this regard. The teachers in Nicolette's Honors Seminar (the class was team taught), for example, realized midway through the course that students needed assistance learning to write main claims about art and philosophy, so they conducted a workshop on and provided examples of effective thesis statements.

When Nicolette reached her nursing classes in her junior year, nearly all of her instructors gave multiple examples of target texts and formats to assist the nursing students in learning to write the medical genres they would be faced with in a workplace setting. During her first semester of nursing classes, she explained that she was learning to write the new nursing genres through "a lot of examples": "They give you blank formats that you can follow and they explain a lot of abbreviations and wording and when it's appropriate to write, um, kind of like medical shorthand and when you should be writing a full narrative, things like that." The nursing instructors seem to value and spend a lot of time with examples and formats: "[The health assessment lab instructor] goes the most over how to write certain things. Almost our entire two-hour lab will be spent on how to write different assessments or plans or what they call 'SOAP notes.'" Nicolette and the other nursing students were provided with a large textbook that explains terminology (lexis) and diagnostic terms, content that is not taught so overtly in many other disciplines.

Nicolette argued that these examples and overt instructions in new genres, formats, and lexis were important to her success: "If they hadn't provided a lot of examples and instructions, then I would have no idea what I was doing, and [I would] definitely be doing it wrong. . . . I feel like . . . the hardest thing with writing . . . is not getting enough instruction, which is not a problem in nursing at all."

When teachers provided and explained a variety of examples and explicitly talked about terminology and conventions, Nicolette was more easily able to navigate her way through new tasks. Yet, even with all the examples and explanations, Nicolette's success also depended on her own strategies for analysis and learning, which she brought with her and used throughout her varied writing experiences. She explained that she used the examples her nursing instructors gave her by printing them out, bringing them to lab with her, taking notes on the examples as the instructor explained them, and then typing up her notes and printing them out after class.

One common problem teachers face with providing numerous examples and formats is that sometimes students follow them too rigidly and are not able to adapt for new situations. But adaptation and analysis are strong skills that Nicolette uses across courses, and her experience in nursing is no different. She spoke with a working intensive care unit (ICU) nurse who told her that she would "never use [nursing care plans] like you use them in nursing school." This affirmed Nicolette's sense that the examples and formats were not to be followed rigidly but instead "[the nursing faculty teach this way] . . . just [for us] to know what is important, and everything that could possibly be included [in a plan] because you never know, like, with what patient you have, what's gonna be the most important things to include. So, knowing the things you *could* include is gonna help."

To successfully repurpose prior knowledge for expansive learning in her zone of proximal development, Nicolette needed to flexibly use her long-standing set of analytical skills and her sense of written genres, but she also needed examples and explanations about content and conventions provided by the teacher. The more unfamiliar the content or conventions were, the more such examples and explanations she needed.

Peer interaction and feedback—or lack thereof—was often as important as teacher feedback. In many of her general education courses, including Honors Seminar and Western Civilization, she knew few if any other students in the class and found few opportunities to interact or share ideas with them. The teachers did not provide many in-class opportunities to interact with other students, so Nicolette often found herself trying to follow cryptic directions or decipher feedback on her own. In these cases, she turned to people outside the class for help; her roommate had previously had the same Western Civilization teacher and was able to reassure Nicolette when she repeatedly failed the in-class quizzes (which the teacher called "one-minute essays"). She often shared her writing with her mother when she felt her mother had expertise to bring to bear (e.g., on an e-mail she wrote to a school principal). However, in Honors Seminar, she was not able to turn to her family or her friends for help; most of her friends were science students who were not enrolled in honors liberal arts courses, and the content of the seminar papers was not content she felt comfortable discussing with her family. When she could not turn to peers for support and feedback, she seemed to experience intensified difficulty with the writing challenges.

The converse was also true. In her junior year, Nicolette found that her nursing classes not only supported but also nearly *required* group collaboration to complete all the new and complex tasks. Her nursing classmates used their Facebook page to remind one another of assignments and due dates and to share Quizlet note cards (i.e., online, student-created flashcards), among other things. She suggested that without working as a group, students would not be able to complete the many tasks required of them: "There's just so much to remember to bring, to do—just so many things to remember; it would be impossible to do it without a lot of people contributing."

Implications for Practice

Going into her college course work, Nicolette had well-developed analytical skills, a flexible sense of how written genres work, and a strong sense of the need for written examples of new text types; she asked questions, always looked carefully at whatever directions she was given, considered what her audience might expect, and responded religiously to teacher feedback, however cryptic it may be. These seem to be the characteristics of successful writers everywhere (not just student writers). But these skills and behaviors only got her so far when she did not have a significant amount of prior declarative knowledge (knowledge about) of the content and the conventions in a particular class. Her ability to repurpose what she knew for expansive learning was often constrained by the ways that the assignments were framed and responded to. Much of what was *hard* for her was related to declarative knowledge about the specific course content and the way disciplinary specialists write about that content, but most of what got *said* to her by her general education teachers was about surface-level errors and mysterious and rigid procedures.

Nicolette repeatedly found herself in a zone of proximal development during her first five semesters of college; in that space, she needed textual examples and teacher feedback that focused not on surface-level issues but on the knowledge, conventions, and expectations of the people who read, study, and write about art, philosophy, history, and nursing. She needed expert instruction about the ideas of the course, how experts in the discipline talk about those ideas, what appropriate texts look like, and how to revise her texts to create a closer approximation of acceptable and expert texts. She also needed to work through challenging ideas and problems with peers and family.

Nicolette's experiences suggest several principles regarding the affordances that students need in order to draw on and repurpose prior knowledge to learn and do something new.

First, rhetorical strategies and knowledge about how to analyze sample texts and their conventions are important to help students tackle difficult rhetorical problems and are an important part of useful transfer of knowledge. The ability to do these things enabled Nicolette to act when presented with a challenging task, even without direct instructor support and feedback. Her ability to extrapolate principles by analyzing examples gave her a smaller target to aim for so that when she wrote a new text she could, as Mel Gibson says in the movie *The Patriot*, "aim small, miss small." If our students do not know how to conduct such analysis, we can spend class time teaching them by providing them examples and showing them the features of the examples we want them to emulate. Some teachers fear this might lead to plagiarism or lack of creativity, but learners can't act in any meaningful way without some targets at which to aim.

Second, the ability to find and usefully analyze examples is necessary but not always sufficient when the task is challenging, because the content is new and/or the task is embedded in an entirely new (to the student) context. If students have no familiarity with art, for example, then simply seeing some examples of good papers is not going to quickly result in their own ability to write good papers. First, students must become familiar with ideas about art and how disciplinary specialists talk and write about art. Teachers need to be patient and recognize that writing improves when content knowledge improves, as long as examples are given and instructions about relevant expectations are made plain.

Third, teachers need to provide feedback to learners, but not all feedback is helpful. Some feedback can actually have the unintended consequence of limiting learning and focusing students' attention on the wrong things. As students learn new material, teacher comments should be intended to help students learn the material better. Once students understand the material, then teacher feedback can more usefully focus on appropriate conventions and language. Giving feedback that is rigid and focused on making a paper appear correct takes students' attention away from learning about new ideas.

By studying and better understanding the experiences of our students, we can continue to revise and improve our teaching practices to successfully teach for transfer and expansive learning.

References

Bærentsen, K., & Trettvik, J. (2002). An activity theory approach to affordance. *NordiCHI: Proceedings of the Second Nordic Conference on Human-Computer Interaction*, 51–60.

Devlin, D., Gordon, M., and Levinsohn, G. (Producers), & Emmerich, R. (Director). (2000) *The Patriot* [motion picture]. United States: Columbia Pictures.

Engeström, Y. (1987). *Learning by expanding: An activity-theoretical approach to developmental research*. Helsinki, Finland: Orienta-Konsultit Oy.

Obukhova, L. F., & Korepanova, I. A. (2009). The zone of proximal development: A spatiotemporal model. *Journal of Russian and East European Psychology, 47*(6), 25–47.

Perkins, D., & Salomon, G. (1992). Transfer of learning. In T. N. Postlethwaite & T. Husen (Eds.), *International encyclopedia of education* (2nd ed.). Oxford, UK: Pergamon. Retrieved from http://jaymctighe.com/wordpress/wp-content/uploads/2011/04/Transfer-of-Learning-Perkins-and-Salomon.pdf

Prior, P., & Shipka, J. (2003). Chronotopic lamination: Tracing the contours of literate activity. In C. Bazerman & D. Russell (Eds.), *Writing selves/writing societies* (pp. 180–238). Fort Collins, CO: WAC Clearinghouse.

Roozen, K. (2010). Tracing trajectories of practice: Repurposing in one student's developing disciplinary writing processes. *Written Communication, 27*(3), 318–354.

Russell, D. R. (2002). *Writing in the academic disciplines: A curricular history* (2nd ed.). Carbondale, IL: Southern Illinois University Press.

Vygotsky, L. S. (1978). *Mind and society: The development of higher psychological processes*. Cambridge, MA: Harvard University Press.

14

CODA

Writing Transfer and the Future of the Integrated University

Randall Bass

Two Paradigms of Education

The idea of transfer is at the heart of the problem of learning; and the problem of learning is at the heart of the future of higher education. The digital revolution has raised new and pointed questions about the aims and purposes of education and, in turn, the capacity of higher education to meet the needs of learners. The matter of "writing transfer" sits in the very center of these questions. In the introduction to this book, Jessie Moore wrote, "Ultimately, this brief volume aims to make writing transfer research accessible to administrators, faculty decision makers, and other stakeholders across the curriculum who have a vested interest in preparing students to succeed in their future writing tasks in academia, the workplace, and their civic lives" (p. 2). The research presented here, and its consequences, not only makes a case for the practices and structures that support writing transfer but also, complementarily, points to ways that writing transfer in turn supports the most important dimensions of learning that universities will need to emphasize going forward if they are to be effective in the new learning ecosystem.

Although questions of access, relevance, and the impact of higher education have been at stake through many waves of debate and reform in the past 200 years, what is different about this moment is the challenge posed to traditional institutions of higher education by the explosion of web-based educational providers and resources, many of which are targeted at learning very particular subjects and skills. As a consequence, higher education is an active space for investment and innovation as never before. Driving this explosion—and the hundreds of millions of dollars of venture capital behind it—is the belief by some that higher education can be "unbundled." The unbundling argument asserts that at minimum, higher education is failing to meet the needs of millions of students (traditional- and post-traditional-age students). Advocates for unbundling argue that institutional higher education can be broken into constituent parts—granularized and modularized into smaller units and stackable credentials. In short, the revolutionary and powerful affordances of the global digital ecosystem—that we can now find information and *learn* new things "anytime, anywhere"—have been taken by many to imply that *education* can be successfully and equitably decoupled from formal boundaries. This is the essence of unbundling.

In the moment of this discourse around unbundling and disruption, there are then operating at the moment two distinct paradigms for learning that represent the single greatest tension of our time for higher education. These two paradigms can be called a *disintegrative* and an *integrative* vision of education. The disintegrative or disaggregative paradigm for learning includes the proliferation of granular and modular modes of learning, often targeted at specific skills, subjects, and elementary competency-based learning. This kind of learning is also driven by the power of learning analytics that can in turn help design increasingly powerful adaptive and personalized learning tools. In this paradigm, discrete learning experiences are ends in and of themselves.

The integrative vision of education is the core of so-called traditional institutions. Here, education is seen not as a collection of discrete experiences but instead as greater than the sum. An integrative vision of education holds that what matters most is enabling students to make connections and integrate their knowledge, skills, and habits of mind into an adaptable and critical stance toward the world. At its best, the integrative paradigm links curriculum and cocurriculum, breadth in general education with depth in the major, theory and practice, and classroom learning with lived experience. These two paradigms are not incompatible, though they are often portrayed that way in current discourse: disruption versus tradition, innovation versus inertia.

Writing Transfer and the Nature of Higher Learning

The central challenge of this moment for higher education is to put the intrinsic power of the disintegrative paradigm of learning in the service of the integrative vision. This is what I (and Bret Eynon) have called elsewhere "rebundling" (Bass & Eynon, 2016). Rebundling is a way to think of a new synthesis between the disintegrative and the integrative that makes it possible for integrative education to thrive in the current context. The issues addressed in this volume speak to many of the crucial issues at stake in the clash of paradigms, as they specifically address differences in the aims and purposes of higher education. That is, are we educating primarily for completion and first employment or for a lifetime of both personal and professional success?

They also speak to what we do and don't know about the efficacy of the university, including one of the most salient questions for our time: Is an integrative education more effective (especially long term) for success and well-being than a disintegrative one?

The research on writing transfer, broadly, and this volume in particular, directly responds to this need for such evidence that supports an integrative approach in many important ways. Designing for writing transfer entails acts of intentionality and integration that speak precisely to what we mean by *higher* education. The five principles of writing transfer laid out in the first section of this volume are animated by the distinctive nature of learning valued by higher education and the unique nature of the communities that compose it. To believe that "successful writing transfer requires transforming or repurposing prior knowledge" through performance (Principle 1) is to believe in a certain kind of learner and the capacity of an educational environment to support that kind of transformation. Similarly, to recognize that transfer is a "complex phenomenon" involving the remixing or integration of previous knowledge, skills, strategies, and dispositions (Principle 2) is to recognize that the development and transfer of writing ability is not a private or discrete act but one, like all meaningful learning, that takes place in situated "social-cultural spaces." Finally, to believe in the intrinsically social nature of writing and communication is to recognize the ways that students' "identities inform the success of their unique writing transfer experiences" (Principle 3). These three principles (transformation of prior knowledge, complexity, and identity) are mutually reinforcing in critical ways and speak to the ways that writing transfer is as embedded in the fabric of integrative higher education as any dimension of learning.

The principles of writing transfer reflect the values of higher education, but they also speak to our aspirations to deliver on those values. In this way the principles that "university programs . . . can 'teach for transfer'" (Principle 4) and that "recognizing and assessing writing transfer require using a mix of qualitative and quantitative methods" (Principle 5) speak to both the need for intentional design and a kind of institutional learning that are too often *not* present in our institutions. To teach writing well for transfer demands several positive behaviors, including connections and collaboration across disciplinary boundaries, appreciation of the complexity of learning from administrators and stakeholders, and support for the application of learning research to the widespread everyday practice of faculty.

The Role of Writing Transfer in the Rebundled University: Four Design Principles

To the extent that these institutional behaviors are unevenly present in our institutional cultures, this volume provides both evidence and practices that point to ways forward—and point to ways that writing pedagogy and writing transfer inform the integrative vision of the future of higher education. At the core of writing transfer are some of the most important dimensions of this vision: integration, connection, identity, and community. Consequently, writing transfer provides us a very rich window into some of the strategies for rebundling our institutions within the framework of the integrative paradigm.

With that in mind, I briefly review some of the ways that writing transfer contributes to a vision of the future of the integrated university. For this purpose, I offer four design principles for the rebundled university and the ways in which this volume's research suggests that writing instruction and writing transfer can contribute to that vision. These four design principles are simply that institutions in the new landscape must continue striving to become *learner centered, networked, integrative,* and *adaptive.* In situating writing transfer in this vision, I hope to provide a bookend to the five principles of writing transfer that are intrinsic to the field with four ways that writing transfer contributes to the evolution of institutions of higher education.

As with the five principles for writing transfer, these institutional design principles arise from the distinctive nature of learning intrinsic to the university and the uniquely complex communities of learners they are. There is then no surprise that there is strong alignment and compatibility here between the two sets of principles. But it might help sharpen the ways that this volume's body of work contributes to the larger project of renewing and transforming higher education to put some of the insights in the context of each of these larger design principles. In each of the following sections, I will begin with the broad institutional consideration and then the ways that writing transfer informs it.

Institutions Should Be Learner Centered: Writing Transfer Empowers Learners

Institutions should be fundamentally learner centered, providing learning environments that support engagement in the context of empowerment and the ownership of learning. This is rooted in the distinctive nature of learning in higher education and the belief that learning is not merely about the transmission of knowledge, skills, or elementary competencies but instead about empowering students with an openness to learning and an agility around learning that enables them to adapt to new situations.

This volume makes clear that writing transfer is not merely about skills or templates or technique but about pedagogies and experiences that can fundamentally empower learners to transform their prior knowledge and apply it with increasing effectiveness to meet a wide range of goals. In chapter 9, Liane Robertson and Kara Taczak made this clear:

> If we want students to transfer what they know about writing to new contexts, they must be able to understand that all writing is situational and that expectations for writing situations must be abstracted before writing *in* those situations can be successful. In other words, students must understand which knowledge to reference and which practices to employ in every situation; they need to be able to frame different writing situations to write effectively in them. (p. 96, this volume)

To argue that all writing is situational is to assert a very high standard to what we consider learning. It implies that writing, like all learning, is deeply relational. To be empowered then is as much a matter of identity as it is of knowledge.

> Together, the course components help students create an understanding of writing within the context of college and an awareness of their writing identity, important for transfer because students most often identify not as writers but rather as students who occasionally have to write for class. By establishing a writerly identity, they can begin to understand their stance as novice writers . . . increasing their chances of successful transfer. (p. 98, this volume)

In chapter 10, Diane Boyd made a similar point in discussing the impact of introducing a relatively streamlined metacognitive drafting strategy.

> When professors and administrators shift their understanding of student writing from a 'performance of a set of skills' toward 'a process that yields an identity cultivated over time,' the ways we assess writing proficiency will become more rich and instructive. Assisting faculty and students to confront their 'stuck places'—in teaching, writing, and life—may be one of this project's most empowering, transferrable results. (p. 111, this volume)

Given the holistic nature of writing transfer, it is clear that what develops capable writers is support that bridges from matriculation to graduation. As Alison Farrell, Sandra Kane, Cecilia Dube, and Steve Salchak pointed out in chapter 8,

Universities need to recognize that they have an active role to play in transitioning *all* students from high school to college. *All* students benefit from structured support when transitioning from high school to college, though the support that universities provide students must be tailored to address the variable profiles and misalignments of particular cohorts and contexts. (p. 90, this volume)

And such support has to be sustained: "Regardless of specific tailoring, interventions need to be sustained and multifaceted, need to recognize the importance of identity and dispositions for supporting effective transitions, and need to be sensitized to take better advantage of prior knowledge" (p. 91, this volume).

Institutions Should Be Networked: Writing Transfer Situates Student Learning in Communities of Practice

Institutions should be networked, with institutional systems and practices maximizing community, inside and outside the institution, and a broad concept of mentoring. At the heart of this design principle is the belief that learning is fundamentally social, whether in the context of mentoring (which can imply a rich network or community of mentors) or more broadly in communities of practice.

Writing pedagogies have long been an exception to the relative marginalization of social learning in undergraduate teaching practices. As Jessie Moore pointed out in the introduction, "Part of the dialogic process of moving from novice to expert involves learning how to learn within communities . . . learning-how-to-learn strategies that apply across contexts or communities" (p. 3, this volume). Learning to write within and across communities is a crucial component to helping students learn to write situationally. "Without rhetorical knowledge and metacognitive abilities," Linda Adler-Kassner argued in chapter 2, "writers tend to want to apply preconceived ideas about what writing is or should be rather than be rhetorically sensitive to their audience and thus miss meeting audience expectations" (p. 17, this volume).

The rise of social learning as a force in higher education has implications for nearly every level of instruction. Among other implications, it stresses that learning is deeply contextual and situational. This is a crucial point because many of the current forces in higher education are stressing scalable and replicable models that are separable from context and generically applied as either standards or templates. Yet, as Linda Adler-Kassner summarized about the Common Core Standards, but more broadly applicable to many attempts to scale higher education,

This agenda implies, in part, that there are generic skills and strategies that can lead to near-universal application. Yet, the research on transfer indicates that it is the ability to analyze the specific expectations among different contexts for practice, whether academic disciplines or workplaces, that contributes to writers' success. (p. 25, this volume)

Writing and writing transfer are critical in a world where social and networked learning is now an integral part of the ecosystem, where, as Rebecca Frost Davis put it in chapter 3, "graduates will increasingly pursue their personal, professional, and civic lives" (p. 27, this volume). In exploring a range of digital projects, ranging from local history to gaming to Wikipedia, Davis argued that networked writing puts students in a kind of communication laboratory that helps them learn to adapt to swiftly changing contexts and multiple audiences. This in turn creates opportunities for students to develop skills that can be transferred to jobs and career:

Digital projects, networks, communities, and resources provide ample opportunities for students to transfer their learning—near or far, high road or low road (Principle 1). The authentic, unscripted problems; networked communities; and real-world experiences may lead to consequential transitions for students moving into adulthood (Principle 2). In particular, technological change requires a resilient mind-set (Principle 3). (p. 36, this volume)

Networked environments represent an exponential expansion of the networks and communities that have always contextualized higher learning, reinforcing the need to connect disciplinary practices to larger knowledge communities in which they unfold. Speaking of one student, Justin, in her case study in chapter 12, Mary Goldschmidt noted that his

sense of these relationships signals the centrality of identity in the transfer process: Consequential transitions are successfully negotiated when the individual can see himself or herself as a member of the new community of practice. All but one of the senior participants described the importance of weekly meetings with thesis advisers and the presence of mentors, experience in submitting proposals for conferences, intentions to publish and awareness of peers who have been published, and participation in joint faculty–student research projects. (p. 127, this volume)

Putting it even more succinctly, Goldschmidt made the important point that "it is self-identification as a practitioner in the field—not the template— that enables [writing] proficiency" (p. 126, this volume).

Whether in problem-based general education courses, undergraduate research, or other high-impact practices or in digital networked spaces, giving students "a sense of writing as *action within a community*" (p. 129, this volume) is a crucial component to maximizing the social and intellectual complexity of institutions as sites of higher learning.

Institutions Should Be Integrative: Writing Transfer Enables Connections Across Experiences

Institutions should be integrative, with institutional systems and practices serving to maximize connections and coherence. Universities are complex communities that represent a density of intellectual depth. They offer an unparalleled opportunity for creating connections across disciplines and experiences, including in the context of complex challenges.

Integration is a central goal of education because it addresses the complex nature of learning both across diverse experiences and over time (what we might call the "arc of learning"). If you believe in an integrative paradigm for learning, then you need integrative tools, sites, and pedagogies to make an integrative education possible. This is where Kathleen Yancey sees the power of ePortfolios:

> If we want students to transfer, they need a curricular site where they can engage in such synthesis, such transfer thinking, and the reflection contextualizing it. Typically, colleges and universities do not offer such a site, which for purposes of transfer involving multiple contexts would need to be a site (a) accommodating multiple kinds of writing, (b) occurring at the intersection of multiple sites of writing, and (c) continuing throughout the life of a student's career; the ePortfolio is ideally equipped to serve this purpose. (p. 45, this volume)

Peter Felten made a similar point in chapter 5 in discussing the role of writing on high-impact practices (and vice versa), arguing that developing writing transfer in the context of integrative high-impact learning experiences leads to the highest and most durable form of learning that David Perkins (2008) called "proactive knowledge." Writing helps students in

> integrating their learning from that context with their other academic experiences, their professional aspirations, and their evolving sense of identity . . . integrative learning is likely to happen when students are supported in narrating their own stories about struggle and persistence in complex environments, developing proactive knowledge in the process. (p. 55, this volume)

Activating this kind of knowledge through high-impact practices again highlights the holistic and integrative nature of writing transfer. Speaking of intercultural and global contexts for writing transfer in chapter 6, Brooke Barnett, Woody Pelton, Francois Masuka, Kevin Morrison, and Jessie Moore suggested,

> Learning to ask questions about new writing contexts also prepares students to inquire about the social–cultural diversity among those contexts. Asking, "Who is my audience, and what do I know about their values and beliefs?" reinforces students' perspective taking, value of cultural diversity, and analysis of global systems. Asking, "What is my purpose, and what writing tools will best enable me to achieve that purpose given my audience?" prompts students to make informed choices as they "address ethical, social, and environmental challenges in global systems." (p. 64, this volume)

In integration's highest form, we could argue that integration is about the *alignment* of one's actions and commitments. And in this way, writing is as crucial to serving goals of diversity and intercultural competence as a broader sense of integration.

Institutions Should Be Adaptive: Understanding Writing Transfer Informs Institutional Learning

Institutions should be adaptive, with institutional systems and practices supporting internal critical capacities for improvement and agile innovation. Universities should be "learning organizations" that are continuously improving themselves through evidence and communal reflection.

Writing transfer, as this volume shows, is an effective means of institutional learning. By *institutional learning* I mean "any processes where the evidence of learning—both quantitative and qualitative evidence—are accessed, discussed, and acted upon by key stakeholders for the purpose of ongoing improvement of teaching and learning environments" (Bass & Eynon, 2016, p. 65). Writing transfer provides an effective window into student learning both across experiences and over time. And research and assessment of writing transfer is an invaluable lens through which to see the effectiveness of strategies aimed at student success in learning. In their study in chapter 11, Gwen Gorzelsky, Carol Hayes, Ed Jones, and Dana Lynn Driscoll explicitly framed the questions posed to them by their respective institutional leaders:

> Administrators at our four universities had asked about the outcomes of writing instruction and its links to larger institutional concerns. In particular, they posed these questions: What knowledge and skills are students learning in FYW? What knowledge are they transferring—or not

transferring—into subsequent courses, particularly courses in the disciplines? How effectively does our curriculum support students' writing
development? Such questions are pressing, because, like many institutions,
ours must demonstrate to accreditors the effective assessment of writing
instruction. (p. 113, this volume)

Writing transfer is one path of learning research that can inform both
individual teaching practices and, potentially, institutional policy. In Diane
Boyd's case study in chapter 10, the evidence on writing transfer and metacognitive drafting strategies had the potential to directly influence curricular
decisions (in her case, whether to offer one or two semesters of first-year writing). Boyd explained that her role as faculty developer

provides a unique position from which to research these questions, not
simply through the usual avenues of consultations and workshops with
faculty but through orchestrating multi-class Scholarship of Teaching and
Learning (SoTL) research. If students showed moderate improvements
using the reverse outline protocol, I could then work . . . to fold it into
our faculty development workshops and in my consultations with faculty
on their assignment design. Eventually the findings could inform how we
develop and measure learning outcomes. (p. 104, this volume)

One consequence of this is the need to support and reward such research
as an integral part of continuous institutional improvement. For example,
Gorzelsky and colleagues argued that we must "encourage writing programs
to collect assessment data on students' developing genre and metacognitive
awareness, as well as on other aspects of writing knowledge and skill, and
to use it to improve curricula, teaching strategies, and connections between
FYW and WAC and WID instruction" (p. 120, this volume).

One of the most important findings of this volume is that successful
writing transfer begins with and depends on the *intention* to teach for transfer. Teaching for transfer "requires a commitment to transfer as the ultimate
outcome of teaching" (p. 96, this volume). Deepening our attention—and
intention—on how students are learning is crucial to the design of any sur-
vival strategy for an integrative education in an increasingly competitive,
crowded, and diverse learning ecosystem.

Writing a Different Future

There are many ways that institutions of higher learning empower students,
create community, and foster integration. But there are also ways that,

often unintentionally, they disempower students by creating disconnected and incoherent curricular structures and siloed communities. Inasmuch as disaggregation is a threat of the new granular online environment, disconnection and disaggregation is an internal threat to traditional universities as well. As Don Harward (2008) observed,

> All too many institutions of higher education—and even proponents of liberal education—are off-course, addressing only narrowly academic means and strategies rather than the integrated goals and ends that matter to our students and to our democracy. As a result, many of our institutions risk becoming complicit in the troubling patterns of student disengagement.

The principles and findings of writing transfer offer powerful evidence that intentional and integrated practices can foster integrative and durable learning. Although all too often treated as a generic skill, writing and writing transfer are deeply woven into the nature of learning, identity formation, and communal knowledge making that mark the very nature of institutions of higher education. In this rapidly evolving, noisy, and perilous new era of learning, we need compelling examples of theory and practice that can help us put discrete learning experiences in the service of something larger. May this volume contribute to that cause, making writing transfer both visible and viable as one of the most powerful tools we have at hand to make an integrative vision lively and accessible for the widest range of students into the future.

References

Bass, R., & Eynon, B. (2016). *Open and integrative: Designing liberal education for the new digital ecosystem.* Washington, DC: American Association for Colleges and Universities.

Harward, D. (2008, April 15). A different way to fight student engagement. *Inside Higher Ed.* Retrieved from www.insidehighered.com/views/2008/04/15/different-way-fight-student-disengagement

Perkins, D. (2008). Beyond understanding. In R. Land, J. H. F. Meyer, & J. Smith (Eds.), *Threshold concepts within the disciplines* (pp. 3–19). Rotterdam, the Netherlands: Sense.

EDITORS AND CONTRIBUTORS

Linda Adler-Kassner is associate dean of undergraduate education and professor of writing studies at the University of California, Santa Barbara. At UCSB and elsewhere, she works with faculty and students on issues around identification of threshold concepts and the roles that those concepts play in learning and teaching. Her most recent book, coedited with Elizabeth Wardle, is *Naming What We Know: Threshold Concepts of Writing Studies* (Utah State University Press, 2015). She is currently associate chair of the Conference on College Composition and Communication and is a past president of the Council of Writing Program Administrators.

Betsy O. Barefoot serves as senior scholar for the John N. Gardner Institute, where she is directly involved in the development of instruments and strategies to evaluate and improve the first college year and collegiate transfer. She conducts seminars on the first-year experience across the United States and in other countries and assists colleges and universities in implementing and evaluating first-year programs. Barefoot has also authored and coauthored a number of publications including the 2005 Jossey-Bass books, *Achieving and Sustaining Institutional Excellence for the First Year of College; Challenging and Supporting the First-Year Student: A Handbook for the First Year of College;* and most recently (in 2016) *The Undergraduate Experience: Focusing Institutions on What Matters Most.*

Brooke Barnett is a professor in the School of Communications and associate provost for inclusive community at Elon University. Her books include *Multidisciplinary Approaches to Communication Law Research* (Routledge, 2012), *Terrorism and the Press: An Uneasy Relationship* (Peter Lang, 2008), *An Introduction to Visual Theory and Practice in the Digital Age* (Peter Lang, 2011), and *Intersectionality in Action: A Guide for Faculty and Campus Leaders for Creating Inclusive Classrooms and Institutions* (Stylus, 2016).

Randall Bass is vice provost for education and professor of English at Georgetown University, where he leads the Designing the Future(s) initiative and the Red House incubator for curricular transformation. For 13 years, he was the founding executive director of Georgetown's Center for New Designs in Learning and Scholarship. He has been working at the intersections of new media technologies and the scholarship of teaching and learning for nearly 30 years, including serving as director and principal investigator of the Visible Knowledge Project, a five-year scholarship of teaching and learning project involving 70 faculty on 21 university and college campuses. In January 2009, he published a collection of essays and synthesis of findings from the Visible Knowledge Project under the title "The Difference That Inquiry Makes" (coedited with Bret Eynon) in the digital journal *Academic Commons* (http://academiccommons.org). Bass is the author and editor of numerous books, articles, and electronic projects, including, recently, "Disrupting Ourselves: The Problem of Learning in Higher Education" (*Educause Review*, March–April 2012). He is currently a senior scholar with the Association of American Colleges & Universities.

Diane E. Boyd is the director of the Biggio Center for the Enhancement of Teaching and Learning at Auburn University in Auburn, Alabama. Trained as an eighteenth-century British literature scholar, she has been working with colleagues in educational development for the past 15 years. Her publications in the field focus on course redesign for significant learning, amplifying learner and colleague motivation, and threshold concepts in teaching and learning.

Nicolette Mercer Clement graduated from the University of Central Florida in August 2015 with a bachelor of science in nursing. She is currently a registered nurse on a women's medical–surgical unit in Jacksonville, Florida.

Rebecca Frost Davis is the director for instructional and emerging technology at St. Edward's University in Austin, Texas. Her work focuses on the intersections of digital pedagogy and liberal education. She is coeditor (with Matthew K. Gold, Katherine D. Harris, and Jentery Sayers) of *Digital Pedagogy in the Humanities: Concepts, Models, and Experiments* (Modern Language Association, 2016), an open-access, curated collection of downloadable, reusable, and remixable pedagogical resources for humanities scholars interested in the intersections of digital technologies with teaching and learning.

Dana Lynn Driscoll is an associate professor of English at Indiana University of Pennsylvania, where she teaches courses in the composition and Teachers of English to Speakers of Other Languages (TESOL) doctoral program on teaching writing, writing center and writing program administration, and research methods. She also serves as the head mentor for new teachers of writing. Her research interests include writing centers, writing transfer and learning theories, teacher professional development, research methodologies, writing assessment, and writing across the curriculum. She has published in numerous journals, including *Writing Center Journal, Across the Disciplines, Writing Program Administration, Assessing Writing, Teaching and Learning Inquiry, Computers and Composition*, and *Composition Forum*.

Cecilia Dube is an academic development practitioner with more than 20 years' experience teaching academic literacies at the undergraduate level, first at the University of Zimbabwe and then at the University of Johannesburg (UJ). She is a published writer, with several coauthored articles in refereed journals and a coauthored textbook on academic literacy, which is now in its second edition. Although Dube is now retired, her ties with UJ continue: She has been a senior research associate with the institution's Academic Development Centre since 2013.

Alison Farrell is a teaching development officer in the Centre for Teaching and Learning, Maynooth University (Ireland), where she is also head of the university's writing center. She has been directly involved in education since 1994 and has worked in a wide range of pedagogical areas at all levels. She is a founding member and current cochair of the Irish Network for the Enhancement of Writing (INEW). She is also the founder of the Summer Writing Institute for Teachers (SWIFT). Her research interests include composition and inquiry, literacy, academic writing, and collaboration.

Peter Felten is assistant provost for teaching and learning, executive director of the Center for Engaged Learning, and professor of history at Elon University. His publications include the coauthored books *The Undergraduate Experience: Focusing Institutions on What Matters Most* (Jossey-Bass, 2016) and *Engaging Students as Partners in Learning and Teaching: A Guide for Faculty* (Wiley, 2014) and the coedited *Intersectionality in Action: A Guide for Faculty and Campus Leaders for Creating Inclusive Classrooms and Institutions* (Stylus, 2016). He is president-elect of the International Society for the Scholarship of Teaching and Learning and coeditor of the *International Journal for Academic Development*.

John N. Gardner serves as president of the John N. Gardner Institute for Excellence in Undergraduate Education; the founding director and senior fellow of the National Resource Center for The First-Year Experience and Students in Transition; and distinguished professor emeritus of Library and Information Science at the University of South Carolina. Gardner has authored and coauthored numerous articles and books, including *Your College Experience* (Bedford/St. Martins, multiple editions), *Developing and*

Sustaining Successful First-Year Programs (Jossey-Bass, 2013), and *The Undergraduate Experience: Focusing Institutions on What Matters Most* (Jossey-Bass, 2016).

Mary Goldschmidt is a former writing program director and educational developer. Her experience includes implementing a writing in the disciplines (WID) program, teaching composition and literature, and conducting a broad range of faculty development initiatives. Her current research examines optimal design in self-regulated learning instruction for promoting intrinsic motivation and engagement among students in the general education curriculum. With colleagues in psychology, exercise science, and nursing, she is also currently writing a self-reflective examination of a yearlong faculty learning community that explores the practice of "slow teaching."

Gwen Gorzelsky is executive director of The Institute for Learning and Teaching (TILT) and associate professor of English at Colorado State University. She has published articles in *College Composition and Communication, College English, Reflections, Journal of Advanced Composition, Journal for the Assembly for Expanded Perspectives on Learning*, and other venues, as well as authored the book *The Language of Experience: Literate Practices and Social Change* (University of Pittsburgh Press, 2005). Her research interests include writing instruction, learning transfer, metacognition, and literacy learning, particularly uses of literacy for personal and social change.

Carol Hayes is an assistant professor of writing at George Washington University (GW), where she teaches in the university writing program and has served in several administrative positions. She currently directs the GW writing center. Her research within writing studies focuses on writing transfer, public writing, and writing centers.

Ed Jones directs the basic writing program and coordinates assessment in the English department at Seton Hall University. His areas of scholarly interest are knowledge transfer, the effect of race and class on self-beliefs and writing achievement, and issues related to administering a writing program. Since 1999, he has been involved with and helped lead the New Jersey Writing Alliance, an organization that builds bridges between college and secondary composition educators.

Sandra Kane teaches in the Intensive English Language Institute at Worcester State University. She previously coordinated and taught academic literacies courses at the University of Johannesburg in South Africa, where she also directed the university writing center.

Francois Masuka is director of International Student and Faculty Scholar Services at Elon University.

Jessie L. Moore is director of the Center for Engaged Learning and associate professor of English, professional writing, and rhetoric. She leads planning, implementation, and assessment of the center's research seminars, which support multi-institutional inquiry on high-impact pedagogies and other focused, engaged learning topics. Her recent research examines transfer of writing knowledge and practices, multi-institutional research and collaborative inquiry, writing residencies for faculty writers, the writing lives of university students, and high-impact pedagogies. She coedited *Critical Transitions: Writing and the Question of Transfer* (The WAC Clearinghouse/University Press of Colorado, 2016). She currently serves as the elected secretary of the Conference on College Composition and Communication.

Kevin Morrison is the director of the International Center at Macalester College, where he also advises students on study away program selection and assists in the development and implementation of the center's orientation and returnee programming.

Woody Pelton has been the dean of global education at Elon University in North Carolina since 2009. Prior to coming to Elon, Pelton was the director of the International Center at Winthrop University (2006–2009) and was special assistant to the president for international programs at Saginaw Valley State University from 1992 to 2006. Before moving into higher education, Pelton worked as an attorney in Washington, DC, from 1984 to 1992, as an education adviser for the UN High Commission for Refugees serving the Vietnamese Boat People in a refugee camp off the coast of Malaysia, and as a Peace Corps volunteer (ESL instructor) in Morocco.

Liane Robertson is associate professor of English at William Paterson University of New Jersey, where she directs the Writing Across the Curriculum program. Her current research explores writing transfer across multi-institutional contexts, especially the role of particular content in advanced writing courses and its impact on students' ability to transfer knowledge and practice into a range of writing situations. Her recent work is featured in *Writing Across Contexts: Transfer, Composition, and Sites of Writing* (Utah State

University Press, 2014) and *Naming What We Know: Threshold Concepts of Writing Studies* (Utah State University Press, 2015).

Steve Salchak is assistant professor of writing in the Women's Leadership Program at George Washington University. His research focuses on how to best use the first year as both a transition from high school to college and a foundation for long-term growth as a writer. Through his teaching and research, he is working with partners in the United States, Ireland, Bangladesh, and South Africa to support improved learning and teaching and to help build the capacity of local partners to incorporate writing instruction into their curricula.

Kara Taczak is teaching assistant professor at the University of Denver. Her research centers on the transfer of knowledge and practices: Her current project, The Transfer of Transfer Project, examines the efficacy of the teaching for transfer curriculum in multiple courses across multiple institutional sites. This research is the second phase of research reported on in her coauthored book *Writing Across Contexts: Transfer, Composition, and Sites of Writing* (Utah State University Press, 2014), which was awarded the 2015 Conference on College Composition and Communication Research Impact award. Taczak's other publications have appeared in *Composition Forum, Teaching English in a Two-Year College*, and *Across the Disciplines*.

Elizabeth Wardle is professor and director of the Roger and Joyce Howe Center for Writing Excellence at Miami University (OH). She was chair of the Department of Writing and Rhetoric at the University of Central Florida (UCF) and director of writing programs at UCF and the University of Dayton. These experiences fed her interest in how students learn and repurpose what they know in new settings. With Doug Downs, she is the coauthor of *Writing About Writing: A College Reader* (Macmillan, 2010, 2014). With Linda Adler-Kassner, she is coeditor of *Naming What We Know: Threshold Concepts of Writing Studies* (Utah State University Press, 2015), winner of the Council of Writing Program Administrators Outstanding Contribution to the Discipline Award.

Carmen M. Werder directs the Learning Commons at Western Washington University, including the Writing Instruction Support Program, a professional development program for faculty who teach writing across the disciplines. She also teaches courses in civil discourse and rhetoric in the Department of Communication Studies.

Kathleen Blake Yancey, Kellogg W. Hunt professor of English and distinguished research professor at Florida State University, has served in several leadership roles for the National Council of Teachers of English, Conference on College Composition and Communication (CCCC), and Council of Writing Program Administrators. Immediate past editor of *College Composition and Communication*, she cofounded and codirects the Inter/National Coalition for Electronic Portfolio Research (ncepr.org), and she also leads a nine-site study of transfer of writing knowledge and practice (http://writingacrosscontexts.blogspot.com). She has authored, edited, or coedited 13 scholarly books, including *Electronic Portfolios 2.0: Emergent Research on Implementation and Impact* (Stylus, 2009) and *Writing Across Contexts: Transfer, Composition, and Sites of Writing* (Utah State University Press, 2014); the latter won the CCCC Research Impact Award and the Council of Writing Program Administrators Best Book Award.

strategies for implementation, and identifies the key considerations that need to be addressed in the areas of pedagogy, professional development, outcomes assessment, technology and scaling up.

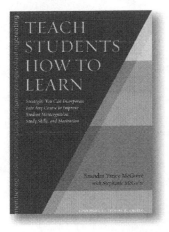

Teach Students How to Learn

Strategies You Can Incorporate Into Any Course to Improve Student Metacognition, Study Skills, and Motivation

Saundra Yancy McGuire with Stephanie McGuire

Foreword by Thomas Angelo

"An electrifying book! McGuire demonstrates how learning strategies can improve learning—and then charges faculty to teach them, complete with the slides for doing so in your class. . . . A must-read—and must-do—for every teacher who struggles with students who don't learn as much as they could or should!"—*Tara Gray*, *Director, The Teaching Academy, New Mexico State University*

"Dr. McGuire's specific strategies serve as paradigms I can adapt for my literature courses. Many of the specific exercises McGuire uses to illustrate metacognition quickly convinced my students that cognitive functions such as pattern recognition effectively guide the close reading of a text while taking time to overview a text and place it in context helps more advanced students take on the challenges of literary theory. The strategies outlined here take away the mystery, not the magic, of writing about literature." **Helen Whall**, *Professor of English and Director of Comprehensive Academic Advising, College of the Holy Cross*

Sty/us

22883 Quicksilver Drive
Sterling, VA 20166-2102

Subscribe to our e-mail alerts: www.Styluspub.com

Also available from Stylus

Leveraging the ePortfolio for Integrative Learning

A Faculty Guide to Classroom Practices for Transforming Student Learning

Candyce Reynolds and Judith Patton

Foreword by Terry Rhodes

"Integrative learning is often seen as the Holy Grail for various learning contexts, such as general education and lifelong learning. It's believed to exist, but it's often unclear how to foster such learning in meaningful ways. Destined to be a seminal text, what Reynolds and Patton provide here is a map to integrative learning through ePortfolios with practical advice leading to real outcomes. I will be providing this book as a manual for those who teach using ePortfolios."

—*C. Edward Watson*, *Director, Center for Teaching & Learning, University of Georgia; and Executive Editor,* International Journal of ePortfolio

"Candyce Reynolds and Judith Patton's *Leveraging the ePortfolio for Integrative Learning* is the most accessible book I have seen about using ePortfolios in higher education. They write this book as if it is their own ePortfolio, providing personal stories and many examples of faculty uses of ePortfolios. The book keeps you reading as if you are listening to the authors tell you all you want to hear about every aspect of defining your ePortfolio's campus purpose to choosing a platform to the structure of a showcase ePortfolio to tips and cautions. I was impressed with their thoroughness and lucidity. Thanks to Reynolds and Patton for this significant contribution to the field of ePortfolio studies."—*Trent Batson, President*, *The Association for Authentic, Experiential and Evidence-Based Learning*

High-Impact ePortfolio Practice

A Catalyst for Student, Faculty, and Institutional Learning

Bret Eynon and Laura M. Gambino

Foreword by George D. Kuh

The authors identify how the ePortfolio experience enhances other high-impact practices (HIPs) by creating unique opportunities for connection and synthesis across courses, semesters, and cocurricular experiences. Using ePortfolios to integrate learning across multiple HIPs enables students reflect and construct a cohesive signature learning experience

The core of the book presents a comprehensive research-based framework, along with practical examples and

(Continues on previous page)